2.95

True Treasure Tales

By Charles Garrett

Metal Detection & Treasure Hunting

Treasure Recovery from Sand and Sea

Modern Metal Detectors

The New Successful Coin Hunting

Treasure Hunting Pays Off!

Treasure Hunting Secrets

Modern Treasure Hunting (with Lagal)

Modern Electronic Prospecting (with Lagal)

Garrett Guides

Metal Detectors Can Help You Find Wealth

Find Wealth on the Beach

Metal Detectors Can Help You Find Coins

Find Wealth in the Surf

Find More Wealth with the Right Metal Detector

Money Caches Are Waiting to be Found

Avoid Detector Problems

Gar Starrett Adventures

The Secret of John Murrell's Vault

The Missing Nez Perce Gold

The Missing Nez Perce Gold

By Charles Garrett

ISBN 0-915920-66-2
Library of Congress Catalog Card No. 88-63979
The Missing Nez Perce Gold

First Edition Printing, March 1989

89 90 10 9 8 7 6 5 4 3 2 1

For FREE listing of related treasure hunting books write
Ram Publishing Company • P.O. Box 38649 • Dallas, Texas 75238

Book design and cover illustration by Melvin Climer
Back cover photograph by Hal Dawson

About the Author

Charles Garrett has searched for the missing Nez Perce gold. In fact, he has searched with a metal detector for buried treasure on every continent except Antarctica . . . from the Australian Outback to the Caribbean . . . from the Sahara to the Canadian Rockies. A native Texan and graduate electrical engineer, he introduced discipline to the manufacture of metal detectors and has generally raised the standards of all detector hobbyists. His company, Garrett Electronics, is one of the world's leading manufacturers of metal detection equipment of all types. Known as *The Grand Master Hunter,* he has written numerous books, some of which serve as definitive texts for use of a metal detector. This is his second *True Treasure Tale* featuring Gar Starrett.

Editor's Note

Except for individuals and events recorded in history, the characters in this novel and their activities are completely fictitious. None of them is meant to bear a resemblence to any individual, living or dead, or to any of his or her deeds. The story is set in Northern Idaho which is presented as Charles Garrett has come to know it while hunting there with a metal detector.

Conversation of historical figures is, of course, fictitious, even though it seeks to portray the character of each individual as generally presented by historians.

In recounting details concerning the Nez Perce Indians and their famous conflict in 1877 the author has relied on sources considered reliable. Over the past two decades Mr. Garrett has spent considerable time in the Northwest where he has hunted for treasure with . . . and shared the confidences of . . . many Nez Perce friends and acquaintances. These associations have helped him to avoid stereotypes in portraying Indians of the past and today. He presents each of his Indian characters as an *individual,* which all of them most certainly were and are.

Of course, this entire disclaimer must be considered in conjunction with the note from the author which forms the conclusion of this novel.

Winter 1988-9

Hal Dawson, Editor
Ram Books

To Roy, Wally and all of my friends in the Great Northwest . . . in gratitude for the happiness I have experienced with you over the years . . . and the serenity and fellowship we have enjoyed . . . this book is respectfully dedicated.

C. G.

Grace Erskine

Wonderful, wonderful Willy! What a fine husband he is . . . so strong and so proud. So proud to be a full-blooded Nez Perce . . . so proud to be an American . . . so proud of me and our children.

Thank God!

Except for his intense pride, we'd never have met Gar Starrett and never have searched for the lost gold of the Nez Perce Indians. And, Willy and Dr. Starrett combined their talents and good judgment to save all of us when our lives were threatened.

Such a grand adventure we had . . . and such an honor to search for the treasure of my husband's people!

Chapter One

The young Air Force major squirmed as he sat in the rickety metal folding chair. He wiped perspiration from his brow and turned to the husky man and attractive woman sitting beside him.

"These people are killing us, Willy," he said. "I never expected anything like this! You're supposed to be mayor. Can't you do something?"

The big, dark-skinned man grinned and mumbled, "Crazy Indians! You never can tell about 'em."

"Hush, Willy," exclaimed his wife, who was sitting next to him. "It's not the Indians. It's those deep-breather types who are running all over us. You've got to do something. The Air Force needs to build that new radar station."

And, it was this proposed installation of some new, space-age type of tracking facility that was causing all the commotion at the town meeting in tiny Ruger, Idaho. The high school gymnasium was jammed, and the gathering divided itself quite easily into three groups. The largest was composed of townspeople and nearby landowners, genuinely concerned about the community in which they had chosen to live and raise families. For the most part, this group remained silent and listened.

The verbal fireworks were coming from the other two groups who were keeping the entire crowd in an uproar. Self-proclaimed professional environmentalists, mostly from such faraway points as Denver and San Francisco, were doing most of the talking. They were loud in their opposition to the new military facility proposed for construction just outside Ruger and they were tiresome in explaining time and again how it represented a potential environmental disaster.

"Why are they so concerned about Ruger and Northern Idaho?" Willy kept asking. "What makes them so interested in us?"

"Well, they certainly aren't interested in facts," Major Robert Deane, an Air Force public information officer, explained to Ruger's mayor, Willy Erskine, and his wife Grace. "The same organizations seem to show up whenever the government or private business proposes to cut down a tree, take a little water from a stream or change the natural countryside in any way."

"Deep breathers!" scoffed Grace. Tall and slender, she was imposing in appearance, especially when seen beside the considerable bulk of her large but well-proportioned husband.

"What's that?" he asked.

"Oh, these environmental watchdogs," she answered. "They're so concerned that their precious air or water might be polluted just a little that they won't give business and industry the chance to grow. They don't care what happens to any of us in Ruger."

"There's more to it than that, I'll bet," grunted

Willy.

"I think you're right, Willy," added the young major. "What concerns me now is their absolute lack of interest in permitting America to protect itself by modernizing military installations. They're on us every time we try to make a change. Worst of all, they won't even let the people hear what we have to say . . . like tonight!"

And, it was true that Grace's "deep breathers" were dominating the meeting. The Air Force representatives had scarcely been given a chance to present their case for the proposed installation. Only a few minutes into what appeared to be a reasonable display of facts, figures and environmental implications, the visitors had begun rudely interrupting with questions that often seemed totally unrelated to the installation proposed for construction in Idaho . . . or that pertained to the environment of the area which they claimed to be "protecting."

Willy's face was growing even more ruddy than normal, and it was obvious that he had become angry. As mayor, he was the nominal chairman of the meeting, but he had certainly lost control over it. Finally, he rose.

"Why don't you people from out of town let the Air Force finish its presentation, and then . . ."

This small, but highly vocal, third group at the meeting then entered the fray to shout Willy down. This group was composed of only a few Indians. They were by no means the only Indians present at the meeting. Many of those in the concerned citizens group who had listened patiently to the entire proceedings were Indians.

The small and vocal group of younger Indians sat alone, however. They were attending this meeting with no concern for their hometown but with only one aim . . . to oppose Willy. Simply stated, they hated him. While Willy was also an Indian, his education, desire for self-improvement and worthwhile employment represented fulfillment of the American dream. These younger Indians were examples of an American disgrace. Few of them held jobs, and none worked productively. For the most part, they took advantage of their treaty status to hunt and fish wherever they liked. They wasted their tribal and other welfare payments on liquor and drugs.

Unfortunately, the drunken Indian stereotype fit them precisely. Furthermore, their behavior and reputation limited those other Indians who sought to succeed like Willy.

"Why don't you shut up, Willy, you traitor!" shouted an obese Indian who called himself White Bird after one of the great Nez Perce chiefs. "You've sold out your people, and now you're trying to sell out the town! How much are you making off this?"

His companions raised their voices and joined him in jeering the young mayor.

Willy clenched his jaws and looked around the room. None of these Indians had voted for him, he knew. Hell, they probably hadn't even voted. It was the worthwhile Indians and similar hard-working citizens who kept reelecting him mayor. They appreciated Willy's intelligence, good judgment and his willingness to fulfill a thankless job with such vigor and enthusiasm. Willy knew that if these people – all fine, patriotic, local taxpayers – could only understand the Air Force plan as it had been explained to him, there would be no objections.

The proposed new installation was to be situated on a low mountaintop just outside Ruger. It would be scarcely visible and was vital to a new defense system being installed throughout the Pacific Northwest. Equally as important to Willy – and, to the productive citizens of Ruger as well – was the military payroll that would accompany the new facility. Although not especially large, this payroll would be welcomed in Ruger because it would be regular . . . which scarcely described the major income sources of the community: lumber, agriculture/ranching and tourism.

"This meeting is adjourned for one week," Willy suddenly shouted. "Everybody can cool off, and we'll meet here next Wednesday night."

"What the hell," White Bird exclaimed. "Let's vote Willy down now!"

"Yes, this is highly irregular," proclaimed a tall and awkward looking woman who was one of the most outspoken of the environmentalists. "We've gone to great personal expense to come here tonight to help protect you poor Indians, and it will be quite an inconvenience for us to have to return."

"Then, don't," Willy snapped. "Nobody invited you, and we don't need you big city types to protect us here in Ruger."

A large man pushed the woman aside and confronted Willy. "We American gun-lovers refuse to let you cowards trample on America's grand outdoor heritage," he said loudly. "Just because you want criminals to be the only people to have guns, you're trying to take away land where patriotic Americans can hunt. We patriots have dedicated ourselves to protecting the rights of all hunters!"

"I'm a hunter . . . have been all my life . . . this has nothing to do with guns . . . I don't know what the hell . . . ," stammered Willy. Grace gently touched his arm.

"You've adjourned the meeting, honey," she whispered. "Let's go home."

"Well, where do we go from here?" Major Deane asked as he sipped coffee from a mug in the small house owned by Willy and Grace. They had also been joined by two men who were members of Ruger's city council.

"What about it, Willy?" asked Matt Trainor, owner of the largest retail store in Ruger.

"Hell, I just don't understand," Willy sighed.

"We all know that the new Air Force radar station won't hurt the environment one bit, and it doesn't affect hunting at all. Those damned outsiders from California and Denver confused everyone . . . "

"And, your Indian buddies kept the uproar steady," added local rancher Rex Thomas, trying to suppress a smile. Thomas was not only one of the area's largest landowners but was Grace's father as well. The local condition of Indian affairs was a continuing subject of discussion – and concern – for both him and the father of his grandchildren.

"No friends of mine . . . " began Willy.

"We know, Mr. Mayor; we all know," Trainor interrupted.

Grace sipped a cup of tea quietly and listened to the men review the events of the evening. A sudden thought caused her to sit up quickly and interrupt the discussion. "Willy," she asked, "what about that man you met in Viet Nam?"

"Who?" responded her husband.

"You know," Grace said, impatiently. "The expert who gave you Marine NCOs the specialized electronics training. You were impressed with him because he knew so much about the Nez Perce . . . "

"You mean Dr. Starrett," her husband answered. "Helluva guy, but what about him?"

"Well, he's an electronics expert and internationally famous, isn't he? " Grace asked. "And, he knows this area. Couldn't he explain to our *sensible* citizens why the radar station is so important . . . how it wouldn't hurt anything? They'd have to listen to him?"

"Aw, I just met the man that one time," Willy said tiredly. "He wouldn't remember me."

Major Deane joined the conversation. "If you're talking about Dr. J. Garland Starrett, I can assure you that the Air Force would be glad to help him remember you," he said excitedly. "He's one of our leading electronics consultants. If he has an interest in the Nez Perce and your country up here, perhaps you could tell him about our problem and the meeting next week. If he's not overseas somewhere, I'm sure he'd be willing to help us."

"Who is this Starrett fellow?" asked Trainor.

"You tell them, Major," responded Grace.

"An amazing person, Mr. Trainor," began the Major. "Words scarcely describe Gar Starrett. He pioneered semiconductor development as a young engineer and became rich. Then, he turned to archaeology where he didn't try to make money but became a legend through using metal detectors in the excavation of historical sites. I know you've seen his picture in magazines. He always wears that old Western hat and a blue scarf around his neck."

"Is he the Starrett who makes equipment to detect metal?" asked Thomas.

"That's right," replied the major. "After using

metal detectors for years, he finally began designing his own instruments for treasure hunting and archaeological use. He organized a company to manufacture them which became the industry leader in all types of metal detection in only a few years."

"I knew that we saw that name on the detectors in South Korea last year," remarked Thomas.

"You sure did!" responded Major Deane. "His security equipment was used in Seoul."

"And, there sure weren't any problems at the Olympics caused by smuggled weapons," added Trainor. "The Starrett detectors worked!"

What Major Deane neglected to mention was that Dr. Starrett's participation in public and military affairs worked just as sucessfully. Supported by sizeable contributions of both time and money, his work on behalf of non-profit organizations as well as governmant and political bodies had made him advisor to kings and presidents . . . military and financial leaders. An international celebrity both in front of the television cameras and behind them, he was admired as businessman . . . scholar . . . adventurer . . . and patriot.

"I'm sure he would help us," Major Deane exclaimed. "Let me arrange for you to talk with him, Willy."

"I'll tell you one thing," the handsome young Indian added. "Starrett is a patriotic American. He was ready to go into the boonies with us in Nam!"

Rex Thomas

That Grace is a smart one; we always knew that. But, getting Willy's friend Starrett down here is about the best idea my daughter's ever had. He wasn't particularly dynamic or impressive to look at . . . about like any other successful big-city business executive. But, that man was something else when he went into action.

He purely wiped out those damned snotty Californians . . . showed them to be money-grubbing self-seekers no more interested in the environment here than our drunken Indians. Those folks liked to have died when Starrett brought out the advance copies of their pamphlet called "Death of a Wilderness." Accused him of being a thief . . . said he'd stolen confidential documents.

Well, it's a good thing he did because the brochure had pictures of Ruger in it and told how the big Air Force "nuclear facility" was going to pollute half the West . . . destroy the Nez Perce culture . . . ruin the hunting and fishing and probably wipe us all out. Not only a pack of lies, but ridiculous to boot!

What it was was a promotional deal for them to mail all over the country. Raise big bunches of money . . . which they'd keep! Starrett made that clear by reporting facts and figures on how they'd done it other places in the past. Showed how they weren't sincere like the Sierra Club or Wilderness Society people . . .

everyone could see plain as day that these busybodies were just out to scare up money for themselves . . . and, scare *is a good word for what the were trying to do!*

But, you know, Starrett never did tell where he got the copies of that pamphlet!

While he was at it, Dr. Starrett put the loudmouth local Indians down good, too. Asked them if they hid from fighting for Chief Joseph the way they'd hidden from the U.S. Government in every war since. Here they were, interfering with the Air Force, and he knew that there wasn't a damned veteran among them . . . while several of the other Indians had served in World War Two and Korea both, and Willy has a chestful of hero medals he won with the Marines in Viet Nam.

Now, the Air Force can build their radar station, and we'll welcome a new payroll into Ruger.

It's a shame Starrett can't stay on for a few days here. He seems to know so much about the Nez Perce . . . their traditions and their bravery . . . that I'm sure he'd love to spend some time with us. Says he has to get right back to Texas where he's working with the governor on acquisition of a big electronics facility for the state. Has to fly back tonight.

Wonder why my son-in-law wants me to go with him when he drives Starrett to the airport in Lewiston? Maybe he's just looking for company on the way back home. Hell, I don't mind. Dr. Starrett is exciting to be with . . . full of stories. And, old Willy's not so bad himself . . . for an Indian, anyway!

Chapter Two

As the big Ford pickup raced down the highway parallelling the Clearwater River, Gar Starrett regaled the audience of two, sitting on either side of him, with tale after tale about treasure hunting, a subject in which Willy had shown special interest. Rex Thomas, was also obviously enjoying such Starrett stories as how the supernatural had complicated his search for an underground treasure vault in Louisiana and how he'd been threatened by Mafia gunmen while looking for diamonds hidden by a famous country singer in Mississippi.

These and other yarns were delightful to hear, but Thomas could sense an undercurrent of tension inside the truck. Furthermore, the tension was increasing as they neared Lewiston. Willy was the source of the problem. While participating in the conversation, he appeared curiously withdrawn.

Thomas felt that his son-in-law had something on his mind, but for some reason was hesitating to voice it . . . very unlike this normally outspoken individual. Starrett also seemed aware of the tension, and he sought to break it.

"What's up, Willy?" he asked. "I have an idea there's something you want to tell me. Let's hear it."

"Aw, Dr. Starrett," Willy muttered. "You're an important person and I know how busy you must be. I just hate to bother you . . . "

Starrett slapped Willy on the leg and growled, "Come on, man, enough of that. I met you in Nam, remember? You were getting me an M-16 and a flak jacket until those officers stopped us. If you want me to do something for you now, let's hear it."

"Well, Dr. Starrett, it's like this," Willy began slowly. And, suddenly, as if a dam had burst, his words poured out. "I'd like for you to go treasure hunting with me. Grace and I think we know where the Nez Perce Indian tribe hid its cache of wealth. We need an expert like you to help us find it. There should be a fortune waiting there."

Starrett was aware that the Nez Perce Indians of a century past had possessed gold in quantities far greater than that of any other Indian tribe in the United States. In fact, he realized that most other American Indian tribes actually owned little real wealth at all. Their "treasure" caches consisted of various talismans and other objects considered sacred and, therefore, valuable only to them.

Yes, the Nez Perce of a century ago had possessed gold in large quantities. Starrett knew from fellow treasure hunters that caches of it were still being recovered occasionally. He was also aware that historians had carefully researched and presented the entire story of the Nez Perce War and that the tribe's history had been well documented, but for a single exception

. . . nobody could ever account for the *missing Nez Perce gold!*

The thoughts of all this flashed across Starrett's memory as he remained silent for a moment before responding to Willy's plea, and there was a smile in his voice as he spoke. "When you tell me that you need me, Willy . . . how can I say no . . . especially to helping out in a treasure hunt. You don't know how much I enjoy that! The only problem is that I can't get back here to start for a few weeks. Will that be soon enough?"

Willy beamed, and his father-in-law chuckled.

"I'm no treasure hunter, Willy," the rancher said. "Why did you want to include me in on all this."

"Well, Rex, it's this way," Willy chortled. "Where I believe the cache is hidden is on your property, so you own a rightful share now. If there's a few million in gold hidden in a cave on your land, we'll sure want you in on the deal."

Thomas laughed. "I guess you will, won't you, Willy? Heck, you and Grace and Dr. Starrett might as well go ahead and dig up that crop of gold. I don't harvest much else off my ranchland nowadays."

Starrett wasn't listening. He was looking straight ahead through the truck's windshield, but Thomas could tell that his mind was miles away . . . a century in the past, it turned out. "A cave, huh, Willy," he exclaimed. "Are you thinking of Rocky Canyon near Tolo Lake?"

"You know about it!" Willy said, delightedly.

"Sure," Starrett answered. "I've talked with my old friend Roy Lagal over in Lewiston many times about the Nez Perce gold and where it might have been hidden. I've even tried to get Roy to go looking for it with me, but he's always had too many other projects to work on . . . and better ones at that . . . caches that were easier to find. 'Sure things,' he calls them."

"I've heard about Roy, and even read some of his books," responded Willy.

"He's a dandy, all right," Starrett laughed, "and he's the reason for my interest in the Nez Perce. We've never gone hunting for any of the tribal caches, though. I'm honored that you as a Nez Perce think I can help you find the missing wealth of your ancestors."

"Gosh, Dr. Starrett . . . "

"The name is Gar, Willy . . . and that goes for you too, Rex. Only governors are required to address me as Dr. Starrett!"

The three men laughed as the big truck rolled down the highway by the river toward Lewiston. As they looked ahead to the treasure hunt before them, the mental clocks of all three were turning back more than a century, back to the time in 1877 when Chief Joseph and a small band of Nez Perce Indians were almost successful in their defiance of the entire United States Army. Gar, Rex and, especially, Willy . . . each had his own ideas about the celebrated dash of the Nez Perce from the Ruger area in Idaho down into Wyoming and up through Montana almost to Canada.

The three men also recalled the bloody events that precipitated this historic trek. Willy knew that legend held one of his kinsmen named Eagle Wing responsible for beginning the bloodshed that had ended almost a century of peace. Unlike other Western Indian tribes, the Nez Perce had not only endured the explorers, settlers, miners and soldiers who had steadily encroached on their beautiful lands. They had prospered along with them over a broad area that included parts of Idaho, Oregon and Washington. And, it was these white "invaders" who had furnished the gold to make the Nez Perce one of America's wealthiest Indian tribes.

The story of how a successful and peaceful Indian tribe had engaged the government of the United States in such an "extraordinary" adventure forms the closing chapter in the history of the Indian Wars on the American frontier. And, this history itself is but one colorful episode in an epic tale. Among white men the epic is proudly called "Winning of the West." To the Nez Perce and other Indians – from Cape Cod to Puget Sound – it is a disgraceful tragedy of how their homelands and belongings were flagrantly stolen.

For many years, however, the Nez Perce of the Pacific Northwest had lived in peace with the newcomers to their land. Indeed, they had truly profited from them!

Chapter Three

The Nez Perce brave known to soldiers as White Wolf squatted beside young Trooper Stout and watched the prime source of his people's wealth pass by in single file. A younger Indian named Eagle Wing stood silently behind them. Appaloosa horses bred by the Indians were being sold to the Army and herded into a crude brush corral made by the Nez Perce on their reservation in northern Idaho. As each horse passed by White Wolf and Stout, a gold piece was tossed on the blanket stretched on the ground between them.

"One horse . . . one gold piece," laughed Stout. "That's the way to do it! No damned banks or paper money."

An Army Quartermaster officer sat astride a handsome Appaloosa and produced the coins from a leather bag he held before him on his saddle. White Wolf smiled as the officer tossed down another gold piece and grumbled, "Damn Indians. Not the way Army business should be transacted in 1876."

The officer then shifted position and continued muttering, to himself, "I don't know if I'll be glad to see them go or not when trouble finally comes here. The Nez Perce are peaceful, and they sell us fine horses." Eagle Wing took a step toward the officer, and White Wolf's smile vanished as he reached up to lay a calming hand on the younger Indian's arm. White Wolf also spoke, almost to himself, "No trouble . . . not going anywhere . . . mountains have enough land for everybody."

If only that had proved to be true!

"Huh?" asked Stout. The young trooper, new to the West and new to the Army, was blissfully unaware of the drama being enacted around him. He understood little about the life of a soldier in these last days of the Indian Wars, but was soon to learn. What Stout did understand was horses, and he loved them. Son of a Confederate cavalryman who had ridden with Jeb Stuart and died at Chancellorsville, the boy had literally grown up astride a horse as he helped his mother manage their farm in Northern Virginia. When his new stepfather sold the farm and moved the family to Richmond, young Stout migrated north and donned the hated blue uniform of the U.S. Cavalry.

"I ain't a Yankee soldier as much as I'm a horseman," he continually told himself. And, it was true that young Stout had never himself fired a weapon in anger.

"Protecting" settlers from the Nez Perce was an easy task for Stout and his fellow soldiers. Relations between these Indians and all white men had been good since the natives greeted the Lewis and Clark expedition in the fall of 1805 as it emerged from the Bitterroot Mountains weary and half-starved. The explorers were warmly welcomed by the Nez Perce. They were fed and made comfortable, and an awesome language barrier was overcome as the travelers learned from the natives the nature of the lands they were crossing and the routes they should take when they continued by canoe to complete their historic trek to the Pacific Ocean.

Such a friendship developed that Lewis and Clark left the horses of their expedition in the care of the Nez Perce, to be repossessed when they returned eastward a year later. The explorers described these Indians as proud and haughty, yet willing to be instructed, and depicted them generally as a quiet and civil people. The journals of Lewis and Clark leave the impression that of all the Indians they encountered, the Nez Perce were their favorites. The peace they made on the banks of the Clearwater River was to last for seventy years.

The Nez Perce were the only Indians that young Trooper Stout had ever really known, but he too was fond of them because he respected their horsemanship and their success in developing the Appaloosa breed. He didn't realize that the Nez Perce were the only Indians known to have practiced selective breeding, but he could recognize the superiority of their Appaloosa stock over the scrawny and undersize ponies he saw elsewhere on the Northern Plains.

"What do you do with all that gold?" Stout suddenly asked White Wolf. It was a question he'd never before considered.

"You grow your own food, make your own clothes and don't ever seem to spend any of it," he added. "But in the few months I've been here, you've put away a lot of gold pieces in that poke you carry. What do your people do with it?"

White Wolf again flashed his bleak smile as he answered, "Not tribal money. Each man has his own horses. Those we sell today come from twenty different families. Each does with his gold as he likes." Eagle Wing nodded as he heard the answer to the soldier's question.

"But, what?" persisted Stout. "You don't use no banks, and you don't buy very much. Where does it go? I've heard tell that sometimes you Indians just bury it . . . say that you're putting it down for keeps or something."

The blank stare on White Wolf's face and Eagle Wing's frown convinced the young Virginian that he'd never get the answers to his questions. Stout was especially wary of Eagle Wing. He knew that the father of the young Indian had been killed by a drunken miner, and it was said that only a promise exacted by the dying man kept the youth from avenging the murder. All the soldiers knew that Eagle Wing was greatly admired by the younger Nez Perce.

White Wolf had agreed to help the soldiers herd the mounts purchased by the Army to their fort, and he and Stout rode side by side down the Clearwater toward Fort Lapwai just upstream from the new settlement located where it joined the Snake River. Their younger Indian companion rode ahead.

A mutual respect existed between White Wolf and Stout, based simply on each other's love for horses and their abilities with them. Moreover, the friendly Southerner genuinely liked the aloof Indian and wanted to get to know more about him and his proud Nez Perce people. He'd told White Wolf of the green hills of Virginia and about the terrible war that had devastated them.

White Wolf had ridden with Stout over some of the beautiful country of the Nez Perce, to his home in the Wallowa Valley of Oregon and around the Clearwater and Salmon River Valleys of the reservation whose boundaries had been steadily shrinking since it was first laid out for the Nez Perce by the U.S. government in 1855. The young trooper found the Indian lands to be just as lovely as those he had known in Virginia but far more vast and rugged. The sky seemed to stretch into infinity on all sides. He came to love the lush valleys and the starkly handsome mountainsides as much as White Wolf and was glad to learn from the brave that the Nez Perce had always tried to live in peace with their neighbors. They had been successful in such peace efforts except for the Shoshone Indians to the south and the warlike Blackfeet to the east.

History for the Nez Perce people was closely related to that of the opening of the American

West, with the arrival of Lewis and Clark in their lands constituting a great turning point for them. Before the appearance of the two explorers and their ragged party, the Nez Perce had been a group of isolated Indians living in small, permanent villages and subsisting mostly by fishing. Made bold by their successful encounter with the strangers and their possession of guns, they mounted their fine horses and set out for buffalo country. Soon, while retaining their homeplaces in the beautiful Columbia River basin, they were also semi-nomadic and ranged from the Washington's Yakima Valley to Central Montana.

Following the lead of Lewis and Clark, fur trappers soon poured into Nez Perce country, followed closely by settlers. Treaties were made honorably between the government on behalf of these settlers and the Nez Perce, then broken cynically as farmers and miners invaded the Indian lands in pursuit of "Manifest Destiny" . . . and personal wealth.

When white men broke treaties by advancing into Indian lands, the Nez Perce did not fight but merely withdrew to smaller territories in the higher valleys west of the reservation. As White Wolf had pointed out to the Quartermaster officer, it appeared that *mountains have enough land for everybody.* An incredibly rich gold strike drew miners and their Chinese camp-followers to the Florence Basin in the heart of Nez Perce country in 1860, and the Indians tried to ignore the gold-seekers, knowing they would leave when the precious metal was depleted. Miners were ruthless men, however, whose ranks included Civil War deserters as well as veterans from both the Union and Confederate forces. Many of them had been involved in Indian battles elsewhere in the West. This lawless breed which lived by no rules except "survival of the fittest" and "winner take all" killed and robbed at will. When they stole from each other and the more peaceful, law-abiding settlers, they tried to blame the Indians. Murders of several Indians were attributed to the miners, and still the Nez Perce never retaliated.

The mountains, indeed, contained enough land for everybody.

In 1863, the government sought to reduce Nez Perce holdings from five thousand square miles over three states to only five or six hundred square miles on the Clearwater River in Idaho. Indemnities were to be paid, but many of the Nez Perce denounced the proposition as a swindle. They were right. The terms were scandalous.

The Indians would lose four and one-half million acres and be forced to become farmers crowded on a reservation. When the Nez Perce were finally pushed into signing the treaty, many of their greatest leaders rejected it and pointed out that the other chiefs had "sold what did not belong to them and we got nothing for our country." This "thief treaty" produced at a "lie talk council" planted the final seeds for the destruction of the Nez Perce way of life 14 years later.

Chiefs who did not sign this treaty continued to live with their clans off the reservation. Among this group was White Wolf who belonged to the band of Ollokot, Chief Joseph's brother, a branch of the tribe that lived in the Wallowa Valley west of the Snake River.

As White Wolf rode with his new friend, the Indian was aware of more recent efforts to force all Nez Perce onto the reservation. The mountains no longer contained enough land for everybody. White Wolf expected trouble. But, he could not foresee the intensity of the turmoil to come . . . how the struggle would grow to such an extent that he and young Stout would become warring enemies and try to kill each other the following summer.

White Wolf

The Wallowa Valley is so beautiful . . . especially now in mid-June when summer has finally come to the mountains all around.

To think that we can live here no more . . . to be ordered onto the reservation by the white man's government . . . to be told by the one-armed general that his army will move us by force, if necessary. It is unbelievable.

Even more unbelievable is the judgment of Chief Joseph and Ollokot that we must obey these orders and move peacefully. There are many among us who would resist . . . even unto death.

The bloodshed would be too great, our chiefs tell us. There are too many of the white men. Their soldiers are too powerful. Even if we kill all who are here now, more and more will come. They will always outnumber us. And, their weapons are too mighty. Nez Perce people can survive only by living on the reservation.

How can we live there? Is this survival? Or, is it mere existence that we must endure?

For days I have been riding the length of our valley, up its hills and into its draws. As we round up all our cattle and horses to move them to the reservation, the beauty of our homeland amazes me as never before. This beauty, however, is hidden today by tears, for, we Nez Perce will never see the Wallowa Valley again as our home. Soon, it will be an alien land . . . the pos-

session of white men . . . a foreign country stolen from us.

We can never forget that this land has been home to the Nez Perce since the first sun rose, and it will remain the home of our ancestors throughout eternity until the last sun sets. After we leave them behind, how soon will their graves be covered with the crops of settlers? Or, will houses and buildings separate them from the Great Spirit?

Yet, we must risk our lives even to reach the reservation as we drive our livestock across both the Snake and Salmon Rivers at flood tide. It is good that there will not be room for all of these animals on the reservation, because there is no way we can get them all across both rivers. Some may drown, but many will escape to return to this beautiful valley to be with our ancestors.

There are times that I envy these cattle and horses who can remain here in this wild and lovely country.

Yet, I will obey our chiefs. They are great leaders, and we must respect their wisdom. But, I know that many of the younger Nez Perce do not honor them. They prefer to fight and await only guidance from anyone who will lead them.

May this leader never present himself to them! The history of our people has been so joyous. A battle with the white man's army would destroy our way of life. Not only would many of us die but such a battle would spell the the end of our history . . . in great tragedy.

I pray that our young braves will recognize the white man's power and listen to the wisdom of Chief Joseph.

Eagle Wing

Our chiefs are old women. They have no heart or soul. They care no longer to uphold the honor of our people. The time has come to fight. We can defeat the white man's army because we have his weapons and we know the country. More important, our bravery is greater than his. Sitting Bull of the Sioux joined with Crow and Cheyenne warriors to kill the gallant yellow-haired general and all his soldiers. Can the Nez Perce be less courageous and valiant when facing a cripple?

No! Then why do Chief Joseph and his brother obey the one-armed general who orders us to leave our homes in the Wallowa Valley. How can our leaders command us to move to the reservation where there is scarcely enough land even for the Nez Perce who live there now. What about our cattle and horses? How can anyone truly expect us to live as farmers? Do they believe we will not fight?

There is no life for me on the reservation! I am certain that other young braves . . . and old ones, as well . . . would prefer death in battle to living as farmers and servants of the white man. The Nez Perce are not reservation Indians.

We have been kind the white men. We have welcomed them to our homeland and befriended them. We have helped them to survive in the wilderness. How have they repaid us? These newcomers have not only stolen our land, they have taken our possessions as they desired them. They are welcome to the yellow metal they dig from the ground, but they take our land as well. And, Indians have been murdered, yet the white man's law refuses to punish the killers . . . even the treacherous miners whom the white settlers themselves despise and fear.

Our homeland . . . once so vast and beautiful . . . has steadily been stolen from us. Now, we are ordered to leave it and the graves of our ancestors forever.

No!

Perhaps I will die. Is that so terrible? Then, my spirit can remain eternally here in the beautiful Wallowa Valley.

If only Chief Joseph or Ollokot would lead us against the white man's army. We can defeat them. Will White Bird be our war chief? Chief Looking Glass? Or, perhaps some other leader we do not yet know . . .

Chapter Four

The Nez Perce sought no new leaders as they met at their ancient gathering place near Tolo Lake. The bad times of the river crossings were behind them, and they were assembling to move northward to the reservation.

The crossings of the Snake and Salmon Rivers had been arduous. Following two weeks of roundup, the clans and their animals found themselves on the west bank of the Snake, facing a quarter-mile of icy torrent swollen by spring rains and melting snow. The Indians knew that they must cross these waters and make their way between the boulders over which rapids tumbled. While making this hazardous journey, each family would have to carry all its possessions and herd its livestock.

At the backs of the Nez Perce stood two troops of U.S. Cavalry to make certain that the crossing was completed and that the Indians did not attempt to flee up or down the river. If trouble was coming, General Howard expected it from Chief Joseph, who had originally objected to the move more vigorously than any of the other chiefs.

Yet, disobedience had never been the intent of Chief Joseph or his clansmen. They had eventually accepted the reservation as their fate and were trying to obey the white man's orders. In fact, the young and mounted braves of his clan perversely welcomed the challenge of crossing the mighty Snake. Along with these strong men, however, were invalids, the elderly, children of all ages and the accumulated possessions of countless lifetimes . . . at least, those possessions valuable enough to be taken along to the reservation.

The scene at the banks of the roaring river was one of chaos . . . tumult, shouting and confusion. Cowhide rafts laden with packs were towed into the flood by the most skilled horsemen, with children and the aged often clinging to the floats as they were swamped by the torrents and immediately swept downstream. Often, the swift currents carried them for hundreds of yards before horsemen could pull them to the river's bank. Canoes were used to ferry those too sick to ride aboard the tossing rafts, and young children clung to their mothers, while they were clutched tightly in return.

The strength, bravery and intelligence of the Appaloosa horses was a godsend to the Nez Perce who had bred them. The crossing could never have been completed with less hardy or vigorous animals. No human lives were lost in the adventure, but many of the cattle and horses – especially the young and weak – were drowned in the wide rapids or swept to their death against rocks. Scores of animals escaped the Indian herdsmen to return to their homes in the Wallowa Valley. And, even though the soldiers were assigned allegedly to *protect* the Indians during their crossing, greedy settlers waited, ready to steal those cattle and horses that strayed from the herds of the Nez Perce. Many were taken while the Indians could only watch helplessly.

While still difficult, crossing the smaller Salmon River was anticlimactic after the battle with the mighty Snake. Worn and dispirited, some 600 of the Indians met at their ancient gathering place known for generations as Tepahlewam. On the banks of tiny Tolo Lake and near the head of Rocky Canyon, through which Rock Creek flowed to the Salmon, the tribe rested. For more than a week they were encamped just a few miles south of the reservation boundary, enjoying their final hours of freedom before submitting to the white man's justice . . . and virtual bondage.

It was a time of peace and sadness on this prairie campground where they had met joyously so many times before. The people basked in the pleasant sun of mid-June and enjoyed the cooling afternoon rains. Young men rode their horses and pranced before their elders and young Indian women. These girls joined their mothers in gathering and drying camas roots for the coming winter's food supply. As each night fell, the youths danced while the older men spent long hours around council fires discussing and dreading the changes that awaited them in the days and years ahead.

Unfortunately, what was actually to occur would be far worse than anyone could ever have foreseen.

As the time for the final move north to the reservation approached, a grand parade was held. While perhaps appropriate, it resulted from no special planning. No great tribal celebration was intended. In fact, both Chief Joseph and Ollokot were across the Salmon River . . . butchering cattle, it was said. By the time they could return to Tolo Lake, the outlook for their Nez Perce people would be far more ominous than when they had left just days before.

While they idled, some of the young men had been drinking liquor. As the days of freedom grew fewer, some of the youths had grown bolder in their talk . . . and in their deeds. They raced the best horses on courses that had been used by their fathers and grandfathers before them . . . yet their races were daring and reckless, like none had ever seen before. They were proud people, and they were not proud of the submission to the reservation that soon awaited them.

With the young men astride their horses and talking of past glories while dreading the bleak future, the grand parade evolved. It turned out to be a formal beginning to the end of a lifestyle known and loved by the Nez Perce people.

Such a small incident!

If a horse had not stumbled . . . if a boy and an old man had not been drinking . . . if either could have remained silent despite pride and resentment . . .

The young Nez Perce men paraded, and the older men watched, along with all the women and children. As the young braves strutted astride their Appaloosa mounts, Eagle Wing's horse tripped and kicked aside a few of the camas roots that were drying in the sun. No harm intended or done, and the young brave was mildly scolded by a few of the older Indians, most speaking in jest.

But, old Raven Claw knew that Eagle Wing had been drinking. Indeed, they had been drinking together and bitterly discussing the events that had befallen them. The older Indian shouted at Eagle Wing . . . and not in jest.

"Clumsy coward," screamed Raven Claw, not only drunk and upset over the move to the reservation, but still resentful from having watched settlers steal his horses during the river crossing. "Your drunkenness ruins the work of women while you should be doing the work of men." Eagle Wing and some other young braves bowed their heads in bitterness and shame while the old man continued.

"If you were courageous instead of clumsy, you would not go peacefully to the reservation." Raven Claw shook his fist in the air. "All of you should be upholding the honor of our people that Chief Joseph and Ollokot have forgotten. And you, Eagle Wing, should avenge the murder of your father!"

The young Indian looked at Raven Claw with hatred in his eyes . . . not hatred for the old

Indian but hatred for the white man. It was not a natural emotion, even for this fiery Nez Perce brave, but one that had been stimulated by whisky. The other young Indian men eyed Eagle Wing with apprehension. They feared for Raven Claw because of the young man's strength and his quick temper, now made even worse by liquor.

Raven Claw was safe even though the eyes of Eagle Wing shown brightly as he looked around him, and beads of perspiration gleamed on his brow. "Give it to me!" he demanded of youth standing beside his horse, then dismounted and jerked the bottle of whisky away from the boy who refused to offer it. Eagle Wing drank greedily and long before turning to his companions.

"Let us young warriors prove to our tribesmen and show the white men that Nez Perce are still courageous people," he said quietly. Only a few of the other youths could even hear him, The other men had forgotten the incident of the camas and were again watching the parade pass by. As Eagle Wing continued hissing a fiery tirade, most of his young companions moved slowly away from him.

"We will show those thieving cowards and murderers that the Nez Perce can be pushed no farther. It is time for revenge." He breathed heavily, both from emotion and the effect of the liquor. His hands tightened on the mane of the horse he stood beside.

Eagle Wing leaped onto his mount and cried

out, "Who will join me to prove the bravery of the Nez Perce?" Almost all of the other young men had moved away by now, and the old people paid no attention to him. Drunkenness and loud talk among their youth, they had learned, was but another gift from the white man.

Only two other braves mounted their horses to ride away with Eagle Wing. Few of the Nez Perce noticed the three young Indians leave the Tolo Lake campground. No darkening of the sun, trembling of the earth or other such natural calamity accompanied their departure.

But, life for the Nez Perce was never to be the same again.

Gen. O.O. Howard

Damn those Indians! And, damn that Chief Joseph!

Don't tell me he wasn't with 'em when the killing started. But, I don't care if he was or not. I blame him because it was his people. They were the murdering savages!

I knew he'd start something! That's why I had troopers with his bunch when they crossed the Snake. We expected trouble then. After they settled in the old campground, though, everything looked peaceful, so I sent the soldiers back to the Wallowa Valley. That's where I thought Chief Joseph and Ollokot might return to make some sort of last stand.

Where the hell did those two go? Damned if I know, but I believe they're back with what few Indians are still left at Tolo Lake. Probably won't be any trouble there now though . . . not enough of their people. My scouts report that most of the Nez Perce have already crossed over the hill south to the Salmon River. Running away, I guess. Well, they won't be expecting soldiers there. If we hurry, we can round 'em all up there and end this with one little skirmish. Get those Indians to the reservation where they belong!

What could have gotten into those ungrateful Nez Perce? We were giving them land on the reservation. Who could have supposed that the young bucks at the Tolo Lake camp would get drunk and raise hell like nobody ever saw on the Clearwater before.

How many have been killed so far? And, don't tell me about hundreds. Get your facts straight! We only know of a dozen or so who were killed by the drunken Indians, but that's too many! And, there's the devil to pay all over the country. Settlers are in a panic from Salt Lake to Spokane. I'm already catching hell from Cump Sherman in Washington. He's afraid of another Little Big Horn.

Dammit, it's not like that at all! And, this isn't like the Nez Perce either. Now, that boy avenging his father with the sorry miner . . . I could understand that. But, not the rapes and atrocities. It sounds more like Comanches or Apaches from down south. The Nez Perce have always been peaceful people, and Chief Joseph promised me they'd go quietly to the reservation. He lied to me. I'll not stand for that.

If the Nez Perce want war, we'll give it to 'em, by God! If we can't kill that lying Chief Joseph, we'll put him and those other chiefs so far behind bars, they'll never get out. I lost this arm in Virginia to preserve the United States as a nation for law-abiding men, no matter what their color. There's no room in it for murdering Indians.

One good thing . . . the Nez Perce aren't fighters . . . damned fine horsemen, but not ready to kill like the Sioux or Cheyenne. We'll take care of Chief Joseph and get the others right onto the reservation.

Call in Captain Perry. Tell him to move out imme-

diately with Companies F and H . . . each man with full field equipment . . . forty rounds of ammunition and cooked rations for three days.

They'll be back at Fort Lapwai long before that. This will be over before you know it. If those Indians want a fight, we'll give it to them. They're in for a good licking before they even suspect that we're coming!

Chapter Five

The Nez Perce not only suspected that General Howard's troops were coming; they were preparing to meet them. Chief Joseph was neither the eldest of the clan leaders meeting around the campfire at Tolo Lake nor was his band of Nez Perce the largest. All of the other chiefs, however, deferred to him. He was the son of Old Chief Joseph . . . his brother and fellow clan leader Ollokot stood solidly beside him . . . he had been accepted as unofficial Nez Perce spokesman in the recent negotiations with the Indian Bureau. Joseph's militance in these futile discussions impressed all the Indians . . . even those who vigorously opposed his eventual capitulation. The other chiefs respected him as their leader even though he had no experience as a war chieftain. None had any reason to expect that he would soon achieve immortality as perhaps the greatest of all American Indian battle leaders.

The Nez Perce encampment at Tolo Lake was rapidly emptying as men, women and children moved some twelve miles to the southwest to a place they called Slapacheap. At the mouth of White Bird Canyon, this new campsite was located where the Indians believed correctly that they would be secure from any surprise attack by soldiers. Scouts had warned that a force of about 100 mounted troopers was approaching nearby

Grangeville where they expected to be joined by a large number of volunteers.

All of the chiefs looked to Joseph for leadership . . . even moreso now than they had in the previous weeks. Chief White Bird's eyes were downcast as he opened their conference by saying, "You know that the young men who attacked the settlers and miners were from my band . . . "

"It makes no difference," broke in Chief Joseph.

"I want all of you to understand that it was no tribal council that sent them out to kill. It was whisky that stirred their blood lust for revenge. I admit that I am hostile to the white man; you all know that. But, you also know that I fear a war between our people and them . . . a fight which we have no hope of winning."

"There will be no battle!" stated Ollokot.

"It is true that we cannot win a war with the United States Army and that we do not wish one," said Chief Joseph. "But, we may be given no choice. We will try to speak with the leader of the soldiers before they attack us. We want to avoid any fight."

The other chiefs muttered, but only one spoke out.

"Chief Sitting Bull and many of his Sioux are in Canada," said Chief Looking Glass. "Let us depart this country and join them there. Let us go now."

"And leave our land . . . "

"What would be do in Canada?"

"How about our women and children?"

"Quiet!" ordered Chief Joseph. "Looking Glass speaks wisely. We may yet flee the soldiers with all of our people and possessions. But, this would be a difficult task. First, we will talk with the one-armed general and try to reason with him and the other white men. Now, let us join our people on White Bird Creek and prepare for the battle with soldiers that may be necessary."

As the other chiefs moved away, Joseph beckoned to his brother Ollokot and pulled him aside.

"I need your help," he said quietly.

"Tell me how I can help you, Joseph, and I will."

The two brothers walked away from the campfire toward the small lake which reflected the setting sun.

"We will never again see this country, my brother," began the older Indian.

"Do not say that, Joseph. Perhaps you can reason with the white men."

"No," Joseph shook his head. "They have always wanted our lands. Now, they seek to punish us as well. I fear that our only choice will be fighting, followed by flight to Canada."

"And leave behind our beautiful homeland," Ollokot cried out.

"It is no longer ours," replied Joseph. "But, that is not all that we must leave behind. There is no way that we can take all of our possessions.

Our flight must be swift."

"That is true," said Ollokot. "Each of us can take only those things that are most important."

"Among that which must be left behind is the wealth of our people," Joseph said quietly. "You know that many of them have left their treasure with me."

"It is only gold," sneered Ollokot. "We cannot eat or plant it. Our people have never lusted for gold. Let's put it down for keeps and forget it! Why should we consider the yellow metal so important now?"

"It is not today about which I am thinking, my brother," Joseph answered. "When we are in an alien land, who knows what we will find? Our people will need all their gold."

"Then, we take it with us and . . . "

"No," Joseph said forcefully. "You do not know the size of this treasure. It is too large. Many families have entrusted their wealth to me. Also, it is so valuable that we cannot risk it to the dangers of the trail. We must hide this treasure . . . here, tonight."

"How can I help?" Ollokot asked.

"My brother, the treasure must be hidden, and only you would I ask to share this responsibility," Joseph said solemnly. "I must go to prepare our people for tomorrow's battle, and I want you to hide the gold. It is loaded on those pack horses over there. You should be able to find a hiding place large and secure enough somewhere nearby, perhaps in Rocky Canyon. I must leave now to cross the mountain to be with our people. It is urgent that we all be ready for the fight I expect when the soldiers attack us tomorrow."

"No, Joseph! Let there be no battle. You can stop it."

"I fear we have no choice," Joseph replied. "The soldiers and the other white men are ready for a fight. Hurry and hide our treasure!"

"You know, Joseph, that there is no moon tonight," Ollokot said. "It will be difficult to make a map or leave a trail in the darkness."

"No map or trails!" Joseph ordered. "For now, this must be a secret between only the two of us."

"Why?"

"We cannot say what courses will be taken by our other chiefs and their followers," his brother answered. "Some may already be fleeing or attempting to surrender. We cannot trust them with knowledge of the treasure. It belongs to all of our people."

"What must I do?" Ollokot asked.

"First, find a good, permanent hiding place," Joseph instructed. "Then, mark the spot clearly so that you can describe its location easily to others. But, you will keep the knowledge only to yourself . . . "

"I will tell you," Ollokot interrupted.

"No," Joseph answered. "We all trust you, and it is well that no one else be tempted by this great treasure. Only when we are safely in Canada should you tell me and the other chiefs where our gold is hidden. We can then reclaim it for the use of all our people."

"Farewell, Joseph, I will hide the treasure of the Nez Perce people safely and meet you at White Bird Creek."

"Remember," Joseph said as he mounted his horse to ride away. "Tell no one where the treasure is hidden until we are safe from the white men or in Canada."

Ollokot

For more than three months I have carried with me the secret of the Nez Perce gold as we fled from the soldiers while defeating them in battle time and again. It all began in White Bird Canyon as Chief Jospeh knew that it must. He sought to talk with the Army's leader, but they fired on our braves who approached them under a flag of truce. How could the soldiers know that we had surrounded them?

We killed as many as we desired before letting the others escape and taunting them as they fled over the mountain on foot. We have since continued to defeat them in battle after battle as Chief Joseph has led our people for 1,600 miles . . . out of the land of the Clearwater and Snake Rivers down to the Yellowstone country, then northward across Montana to the Bear Paw Mountains . . . where we rest here 50 miles from Canada. At last we have finally outrun the white soldiers, and they will not be able to reach us before we have escaped to Canada.

We have engaged the U.S. Army in battle more than a dozen times and have never been defeated by them. Our fighting men have displayed great bravery and strength. Chief Joseph has distinguished himself as a leader. The story of our successful flight to freedom will be told around campfires until the end of time.

What will Canada be like, I wonder? Will there be enough buffalo for both the Nez Perce and Sioux?

Some of the chiefs urge Joseph to hurry our people onward. He is wise to wait and let us all rest. The times have been hard, and we are safe at last from the soldiers of the one-armed general. Our scouts only yesterday found nothing around us but herds of elk and antelopes. No enemy was in sight.

I am glad for this safety, for I truly fear another battle. The Great Spirit Chief has been good to me throughout our fighting, but I know that death awaits if we must battle the soldiers yet another time. It is well that our fight is finally over . . .

Strange, to hear the noises of running animals. It sounds almost like a buffalo stampede or galloping horses. And, I can hear men shouting. Yet, I know that no herds are near and that the soldiers who pursue us are still far away. Why do our people scurry about so? And, why is Joseph rushing toward me with alarm in his eyes?

What danger could face us now with freedom so near?

Trooper Stout

Damned if we'd ever caught them Indians if it hadn't been for Colonel Miles and his men. When General Howard realized Chief Joseph had fooled us again and the Nez Perce had got away, he sent a telegraph message for help.

Them other troops come over from Dakota, crossed the Missouri River on a steamboat and cut the Nez Perce off. Only, Colonel Miles didn't know what he was meeting up with. Called for an old-fashioned charge and got a bunch of his men and officers killed. Lordy, I'm glad it wasn't us. We been through enough! Miles and his men had a helluva fight, before the colonel seen he couldn't whip them Indians neither. So, he settled down to hold them there and wait for us while he tried to talk Joseph into surrendering.

This fight with the Nez Perce has been a big thing all over the country. I understand that Old General Sherman called it one of the "most extraordinary" Indian wars that ever was. It's been all of that . . . and then some. More than a hundred of our troopers was killed, and we didn't whip 'em a single time until this last fight!

They say that Colonel Miles wanted the Indians to surrender to him so bad that he was plumb near crying. Scared to death that Colonel Sturgis or General Howard would show up to outrank him and get credit for finally stopping Chief Joseph.

Well, let me tell you there ain't no credit to be had by anyone on our side. I know that them Indians didn't want to fight. They just wanted to be left alone on their land. They was ready to live in peace forever.

But, that wasn't how it was to be. We run 'em off their land and then chased 'em to hell and gone. Just like Lincoln wouldn't leave us Southerners alone, we couldn't let the Indians keep on living the way they wanted to. Now, most of their chiefs is dead. Looking Glass, Ollokot and some others were killed just in this last battle. Only White Bird and Chief Joseph are left, and he's told all of us that he will fight no more forever.

I guess the war is finally over. The Nez Perce can live in peace again.

Chapter Six

After a century of such "peaceful living," common goals of some of today's Indian descendants of the Nez Perce War could be described in three words – beer, marijuana and fishing. "Fat, drunk, unambitious, stoned or all of the above" was the way Willy described the current lifestyle of too many of his fellow Indians to Gar Starrett as they again drove between the Lewiston airport and Ruger. Almost a month had passed since Starrett's first visit to the community. He was now honoring his pledge to return to help Willy look for the missing tribal gold. The famed treasure hunter had talked several times by telephone with Willy and Grace and was eager to join them in their search.

"Yet, you tell me you're a full-blooded Nez Perce, Willy. You don't fit in any of those categories," commented Starrett.

"And, I'm not alone," Willy replied. "There are plenty of other Indians who work hard and contribute to their communities. Unfortunately, there are a few who won't even try. And, they attract the public's attention!"

"What makes you different from them?" Starrett asked.

"Just lucky I guess." The handsome Indian turned to his new friend and grinned.

Then his face grew somber as he continued, "Even though it didn't seem so lucky at the time when I was growing up in different foster homes."

"So, you weren't raised by Indians?" Gar asked.

"No, and somehow at least one of those sets of foster parents put some ambition in me. A high school librarian and the football coach helped out and the Marines finished the job."

Driving on the highway that paralleled the Clearwater River, they passed a little yellow Japanese pick-up truck parked at the river's edge with three Indians in the back. Two were lying down and one sat on the tailgate. All three were obviously overweight, naked from the waist up and drinking beer. As Willy and Starrett passed the small truck, one of the Indians who had been lying down sat up and waved a large salmon, another raised a silver beer can in greeting and the third saluted them with a single finger.

Starrett laughed. "Either he's trying to let the world know he's number one, or he's telling you and me what he thinks of us, Willy."

The husky Indian smiled as he replied, "Aw, that's just old Bareass, Gar. He hates my guts."

"Strange name for an Indian or anyone else," Starrett observed as they continued to drive.

"Well," Willy chuckled, "he used to claim that he had an Indian name that meant Savage Grizzly or some sort of crap like that. But we just call him Bareass. It seems to fit somehow."

"Wasn't he one of the main ones giving the Air Force and you such a hard time that night?"

"Yep," Willy answered. "We've known and disliked each other all our lives, or I guess I should say that he dislikes me. I don't give a damn about him one way or the other. If anything, I feel sorry for him."

"You've known him a long time, huh?"

"Yeah, we grew up together. And, he represents a good example of what growing up Indian can do to some people. He's damned smart . . . was a good looking devil before he got fat . . . could have really made something of himself. But, he was always lazy . . . dropped out of high school, dodged the draft and has no skills or trade of any kind. Lives on welfare and what he can steal or scratch up by fishing."

"A real shame," commented Starrett.

"What makes it worse," responded Willy, "is that the other Indians look up to him because he's so damned cunning. He's able to lie, cheat and steal so well!"

The two men rode in silence for some minutes before Starrett asked, "You Indians have special fishing rights, don't you?"

"That's right, Gar. Because of the old treaties, we can hunt or fish anywhere and anytime that we like . . . and any way we want to . . . with nets, clubs or anything else." Willy laughed. "Today's 'white settlers' don't like it worth a damn either."

"I can see where they wouldn't," commented Starrett. "But, you're allowed to hunt and fish this way only for your personal needs, aren't you?"

"Sure, but that doesn't stop Bareass and trash like him from selling some of their fish or game. That even makes me mad as hell, but what can you do? They're so lazy and worthless that they don't catch or shoot enough to make any difference."

The road crossed the Clearwater, and the two men headed south into Nez Perce country. Less than an hour later, they were at Willy's home in Ruger, being greeted by Grace who opened a beer for Willy and diet soft drinks for Starrett and herself. Both men declined her offer of glasses.

"Okay," she declared. "So, Willy is still a crude Indian who drinks beer from the can. But, at least he's dressed and in the living room of our house and not sprawled out half naked on some river bank stoned on grass."

They all laughed.

"Your husband's been telling me about life around here for the noble redman," Starrett said.

"It's no joke to me, Gar," Willy interrupted.

"In fact, it breaks his heart," Grace stated. "You see, Gar, Willy is proud to be a Nez Perce, and he's proud of the grand history and traditions of his people."

"He's doing his part to uphold that tradition," Starrett said. "Fine Marine record . . . running the town here and all."

"You don't know the half of it," his wife stated.

"Oh, don't start all that," Willy grumbled.

"Yes, please do," Starrett urged. "I'd like to

know more about you and Willy."

Willy rose and left to get another beer as Grace began telling of how she and Willy had been fellow officers in the high school honor society and how he had enlisted in the Marines when she went to college. She told of her father's objections when she started dating the wounded veteran after he returned home and was first employed to manage the municipal water plant.

"Called me a stupid Indian," Willy said, returning to the room. "Told Grace I'd never amount to anything."

"Rex Thomas . . . the man I met last month . . . said that about you?" Starrett asked as he shook his head.

"Ha! Daddy's long since apologized," Grace laughed. "Even before the wedding. You see, he kept confusing Willy with some of the other Indians. But, my Willy showed him. Proved how *stupid* he was by going over to Lewis & Clark State College and getting his degree in less than three years."

"What did you study, Willy?" Starrett asked.

"Oh, I didn't know what to take. I was just getting a degree to prove something to Grace's dad . . . and to myself. Since I was working for the city, I decided to study municipal government."

"And, graduated with honors," Grace reported. "Plus, having job offers from cities all over the Northwest."

"But, you came back here," Starrett

commented.

"I'm a Nez Perce, Gar," Willy answered. "I belong here because I want to do things for this town and these people."

"Oh, Willy," his wife said. "Haven't you already done enough by letting them keep electing you mayor after you're already city manager. They've got him trapped, don't you see, Gar. As a budget-conscious mayor, he won't raise the city manager's salary."

"Ah, what do you care," Willy muttered. "You're the only daughter of one of the paleface ranchers who got rich by stealing my people's land . . . "

"And, speaking of your people," Starrett broke into what he assumed was a continuing subject of discussion between the young couple, "we saw two or three of them on the highway today who didn't seem to think much of their fellow Nez Perce."

"Old Bareass, drunk and out fishing," Willy explained.

"Well, he's never been a friend of ours," Grace related, "especially since he tried to harass Willy by blocking his car that night."

"How's that?" Starrett asked.

Willy grinned as Grace began the story of how several Indians had parked their cars around Willy's truck when he was working late one night at the city offices. "So, he went into the bar where they were drinking and politely asked the drunks to move their cars and let him out. They told him where to go and kept drinking. He was friendly and warned them, but they didn't listen. Made him wait until they were ready to leave."

Starrett smiled as he waited for her to continue. "Didn't take him seriously, huh?"

"That's right, just like daddy," Grace continued. "So, a few nights later when the same thing happened, Willy went in the saloon. Again, he was polite and asked them to move their cars. Same tune, next verse. So, Willy goes back outside and the next thing Old Bareass and his buddies hear is windshields being smashed. They come out and found Willy taking a baseball bat to all three of their cars."

Willy was chuckling as he broke in to conclude the story, "Then, that gutless bastard tells his two buddies to take care of me, and they come at me . . . one on each side."

"So, Willy cripples one of them with a kick to the knee and knocks the other one out by hitting him in the head with his baseball bat," Grace continued cheerfully. "Then he starts walking toward their leader and says, 'You're next, fat boy.' You should have seen him run!"

"I told them I'd have a pistol the next night, and I did," Willy said.

"Any parking troubles since?" Starrett asked.

"None at all," Willy answered. "They just say things to try to bug us occasionally, but we won't let them."

Grace frowned. "Before you saw him at the river, I guess . . . he was following me again this morning, honey," she said.

"What?"

"Yeah, Fighting Grizzly himself, and he mentioned the Nez Perce treasure."

Now, it was Starrett who sat up and paid attention.

Grace turned to him and said, "He and his buddies know about you, Gar. He sneered when he told me he'd heard we had to hire an expert to help us find the treasure. Said that it wouldn't do us any good, though, because he'd already made a deal that would let him get to it first."

Gar Starrett

Really, no surprise. In fact, it would be surprising if the Indians around here weren't out looking for the gold. There's just been too much talk about it over the years, and there have been too many smaller Indian caches discovered. I know that Roy Lagal from over in Lewiston has found several good ones around here.

Besides, it's a quick way to get rich. Must look especially good to a lazy Indian who can't realize how much work is involved.

So, what we have on our hands now, apparently, is a bunch of fat drunks who know about me and the effort we're going to make. Maybe that's what has stirred them up! Don't see any special problem there. What I would like to know is what kind of deal *they think they've made that will let them get to the treasure before us.*

Although, after more than 110 years, I shouldn't be concerned about the speedy efforts of Indians to find the missing Nez Perce gold!

Chapter Seven

Starrett had insisted that Willy and Grace be his guests for the weekend at a motel in Grangeville, just east of Tolo Lake.

"It will let us get started earlier in the mornings," he explained, "and you won't have a long drive home each night."

"Plus, it lets me get away from the kids for a couple of days while they enjoy riding horses at the ranch," Grace added. "Let's go treasure hunting more often!"

The three were seated in Grangeville's "nice" restaurant, in a handsome old building with high ceilings located in the center of the small but active town. As the seat of a county that was one of Idaho's largest in size but smallest in population, the town had to provide the needs of a vast trading area. The restaurant's salad bar had been surprisingly well stocked with fresh vegetables. Plus, the menu offered one or two real surprises. The weekend was starting out even better than Starret had anticipated.

"Grangeville isn't on the reservation proper?" he asked.

"No," Willy replied, "just a few miles south. But, it's certainly in the heart of Nez Perce country, especially as related to the start of the war. Tolo Lake, where the Indians were camped when the trouble first started, is only a few miles west, and White Bird Battlefield is just over the mountain. That's where the civilian volunteers with the soldiers ignored the Indians' flag of truce and shot first to begin the war."

"I want to see the site before we go back to Ruger," Starrett said, "but I'm anxious to get out to Tolo Lake early tomorrow."

"That's where Grace is certain that the treasure is hidden," Willy said. "You know, Gar, she doesn't like to talk about it, but my wife is one of the most knowledgeable historians around when it comes to the Nez Perce and the war. After she got her degree in history from Stanford, she went for a masters at Washington State and specialized in the Nez Perce, then did most of the work for a doctorate . . . "

"Oh, hush, Willy," Grace broke in, "it's all book-learning. I've never really searched for relics the way that Gar has . . . all over the world."

"I'm impressed, Grace," Starrett offered, "because I've read some of your articles the past few weeks. And, I know how much hard work goes into getting a doctorate. Plus, don't ever downgrade book-learning. Every treasure hunt must start with research, and lots of it. Without the proper research, no treasure hunt can be successful. Even if you accidentally find something without investigating first, you'll never know what you missed by not checking out your objective completely with proper research. I honestly feel that many so-called treasure hunters leave behind far more than they ever discover and carry away with them."

Starrett nodded his head toward Willy. "I thought that I knew something about your Nez Perce, but the articles Grace has published have convinced me she's obviously way ahead of everybody else . . . and, I'm glad she's on our team!"

"Me, too," added Willy with a laugh.

The attractive young woman smiled and lowered her head to hide her blushing cheeks.

"Daddy is coming into town to have breakfast with us tomorrow before we go out to Tolo Lake," she explained. "He and Willy can describe the lay of the land to you."

"What I'm interested in right now is history and how your opinions reflect upon it," Starrett said, "so, let me fire the questions, and you answer. Because I'm an inquisitive cuss, you'd better be ready to back up your opinions."

"Oh, don't worry, Gar," Willy said. "Grace has enough opinions for all of us."

"Hush," she demanded.

"First, why Tolo Lake?" Starrett began. "Why didn't Chief Joseph and the others leave their treasure in the Wallowa Valley? Why take a chance on losing it at that dangerous Snake River crossing?"

"Remember, Gar," she answered, "they thought they were going to the reservation . . . and, that they were going to live there. When they left the Wallowa Valley and crossed the Snake and Salmon, they planned to move peacefully and not come back. There was no need then to leave the treasure behind or to hide it."

She smiled at Starrett before continuing. "I imagine that you already know about the good-sized cache that was accidentally bulldozed up just a year or so ago by construction crews who were enlarging a spring near the crossing site on the Snake?"

"I know what you wrote about it in that historical quarterly," Starrett answered. "And, circulating among professional treasure hunters is the story of another Nez Perce who recently found a $20,000 cache near the same spring and was spending $20 gold pieces over in Pendleton. But, tell me again why you're so sure the bulldozed cache of gold wasn't the tribal treasure."

"Not nearly big enough," she replied quickly. "Besides, Gar, when they were so busy crossing that flooded river, those Indians wouldn't have had the time to bury a large cache properly. One or more of the families must have left their gold in the soft ground there by the spring. Remember, too, that the cache wasn't even buried deeply. Chief Joseph would have never left the treasure of the entire tribe in such a vulnerable spot."

"Well thought out," Starrett replied. "Okay, then, why Joseph's sudden urge to hide it when the tribe left Tolo Lake?" he continued. "Since he had taken it that far, why not keep it with him."

Grace frowned slightly as she began her reply. 'Gar, most people believe that Chief Joseph really didn't want to fight. I agree, but I also believe that he'd come to accept the inevitability of war. After the trouble erupted at Tolo Lake, he became convinced that flight to Canada was their only answer. I believe that the cache was just too large to him to consider carrying along."

"That sounds reasonable," Starrett answered. "Anyway, most of the Nez Perce were pretty busy right about that time! So, if the treasure is in the Tolo Lake area, the urge to hide it had to have been sudden. Chief Joseph was there only a day or so between the time of trouble with settlers and the battle at White Bird that began their flight, wasn't he?"

"They say he was butchering cattle," Willy answered, "but, I've heard some interesting stories about where Chief Joseph and Ollokot really were when the killing began."

"Oh, Willy," cried Grace. "Don't bring up those nasty old rumors." She turned back to Garrett and said, "Remember, Gar . . . I think the decision to hide the treasure was made only when Chief Joseph finally realized what was facing him and the Nez Perce . . . I mean, fighting and running away and all. He knew they couldn't take the gold with them. So, I'd agree with you . . . but, I'd also point out that the decision made at Tolo Lake was not so much timely as sudden."

"One of our tribal legends tells of Joseph entrusting the cache entirely to Ollokot," Willy said, "and, asking him to hide the gold. Then, he didn't even want to know where it was hidden himself."

"But, Ollkot was killed in the battle at Bear Paw Mountains . . . " began Starrett.

"Before he'd had a chance to tell anyone," added Grace.

She continued the history of the Nez Perce people, noting that it was years later before many of them ever returned to Lapwai and the reservation . . . if at all.

"Lots of 'em died down in Indian Territory," said Willy.

"Don't forget, too," Grace added, "that Tolo Lake and Rocky Canyon aren't even on the reservation, and Daddy's grandfather probably wouldn't have been very happy to welcome any Indians back to snoop around on his land a hundred years ago!"

"Rex is tough enough on 'em today," laughed Willy.

"Okay, young people," began Starrett. "Let's talk about Indians in general and the way they've been known to hide caches. Correct me if I'm wrong, but don't Indians usually hide their caches in pretty obvious places . . . where not much actual work is required?"

"Nobody really likes work, Gar, no matter what his race or color," responded Grace. "So, anyone who hides a cache tries not to work any harder than necessary."

"Natural places are favorites around here,"

said Willy. "I've known of Indian caches being found in natural holes in the ground or caves and in sliderock. When caches are buried, it's almost always in soft ground. Remember, those Indians didn't have a backhoe to dig with."

"And, Ollokot – or whoever Joseph left the cache with – was in a hurry," Grace reminded them. "We should keep that in mind throughout our search."

"We'll have several metal detectors with us," Starrett said, "including the best instruments in the world today. But, the detectors I use probably won't be as important as our eyes."

He looked up at Grace and Willy. "What I'd like for us to do tomorrow is look around Tolo Lake together and then split up and search separately. I'll handle the detectors when either of you believe you've found something that might require them."

Starrett accepted the check from their waitress as they rose. "But, now I'd like to take a walk back to the motel in this fine mountain air and get a good night's sleep before starting out tomorrow."

Starrett held open the big door of the restaurant, and Grace and Willy preceded him into the night.

Grace Erskine

Weren't we lucky to meet Gar Starrett and have him help us look for the missing Nez Perce gold! He's such an interesting man . . . and so nice. You'd never suspect that he's done all those things or is such an important person.

And, hasn't he been polite to Willy and me . . . showing so much respect for our opinions and ideas! I imagine that he really knows far more about the Nez Perce than either of us, and I'm certainly flattered that he's read those dull, scholarly articles of mine. They must seem pretty tame after the ones he writes for National Geographic and magazines like that!

We could be so close to the Nez Perce treasure at last. But, Willy and I have never even talked about what we would do if we found it. It's on daddy's property, but he'd certainly let us keep it. I think that Willy has some plans about using the money to help younger Indians. In Gar's book on caches, he says that you should always have an understanding with your partners before you find a treasure. I'll be sure to bring up the subject tomorrow.

Chapter Eight

"Watch out for snakes," cautioned Rex Thomas as he led Grace, Willy and Starrett around Tolo Lake. "These aren't your big Western Diamondbacks, but they're rattlers and plenty mean and poisonous. We sure don't want to tangle with them."

Each of the group looked down at the ground and the scrub brush growing there amid rocks of all sizes.

"Plenty of places for them to hide," Starrett commented as he pushed aside a rock with the heavy stick Thomas had given him, "but Willy's equipped to take care of any varmints." Starrett pointed with his stick toward the six-shooter that the big Indian wore in a holster on his belt.

Willy grinned. "Just give me a chance to shoot 'em *before* they bite you and not after."

"Catch them in the forked end of that stick, Gar," Thomas added.

"Oh, be quiet about snakes," Grace exclaimed. Dressed in Levi's and wearing high leather boots, she seemed prepared for the outdoors. She smiled as she looked at Starrett and recognized his two treasure hunting "trademarks," the old Western hat pulled down low on his forehead and the blue scarf knotted at his throat. "Let's talk about Tolo Lake. It's not really much to look at, is it, Gar?"

Starrett couldn't help but silently agree with

Grace. Tolo Lake might be as integral a part of the Nez Perce story as the Appaloosa horse, but as a body of water, it was singularly unimpressive. No trees or bushes surrounded it. Almost adjacent to a paved road, it was smaller than many of the stock tanks or ponds in Starrett's native Texas. In fact, he could visualize a "hobby rancher" driving up to such a stock tank in a pickup loaded with hay . . . ready to call his cattle by honking the horn and, then, feeding them.

As Starrett gazed across the still waters of the small lake, his vision of a pickup began to change into that of an Appaloosa pony, and the rancher became a young Indian in buckskins. Starrett realized that he was standing next to no mere pond. He had never seen a stock tank that made his skin tingle with a sense of living history as it did here at Tolo Lake. He could close his eyes and hear the shouts of braves as they raced their ponies. Conversations of the older Indians seemed to rise and ebb all around him. The women chattered as they spread out camas roots to dry. Even after more than century, there remained here at Tolo Lake a keen sense of the presence of many generations of Nez Perce who had camped at this location over the years.

"What a magnificent site," he thought. "I'd like to hunt here for a month with metal detectors."

All around them, the land stretched flatly for miles. Tolo Lake lay in a bowl in the middle of

Camas Prairie with distant low mountains in sight on almost every side. Tallest were White Bird Hill immediately to the south and Cottonwood Bluff to the northwest, both of which had figured in the Nez Perce War. The lake was between two forks of Rock Creek, streambeds that were dry today . . . and most of the time, according to Thomas.

"Now, Rock Creek itself, over there across the road, may have a little water in it," he pointed out, "but streams around here don't flow very much except in the springtime or after a rain."

Grace walked up next to Starrett and threw a stone into the still lake. They watched ripples spread, and she mused, "I wonder how many Indian children have done that?"

"Hey, you two," shouted Willy, "quit day-dreaming and let's start looking for treasure."

"Well, I can't see that the lake here is any place to begin looking," said Starrett. "There's no slide rock or gullies in sight around here now, and I don't believe that anything like that might have been naturally covered up in the last hundred years. What do you think, Grace?"

The young woman had already begun walking back toward the road. "I agree, Gar," she said. "I've always felt that Rocky Canyon across the pasture there was the place to hunt. Goodness knows, Willy and I have spent enough time looking around down there!"

Thomas helped Grace over the barbed-wire

fence before stepping into his pick-up. "And, speaking of the time you two have wasted . . . I've got to get back to work," he said to them as he closed the door. "Grace knows the country around here better than I do, and Willy has his truck which should be big enough to haul in all the gold you find. Just watch out for snakes!" The rancher rolled up the window of his truck and drove away.

Starrett smiled as he watched him depart before turning to Grace and remarking, "I don't think your father has much hope for us and our treasure hunt."

"Poor daddy," said Grace. "Not only did he grow up searching for the gold himself and not finding it, but he's had to chase treasure hunters off this land as long as I can remember. Finally, he started putting mean bulls in these pastures, and they kept most people away."

Starrett paused to take his eyes away from Grace and look around the pasture as he and Willy began climbing the fence.

"Oh, no," she laughed. "There's no stock around here today. Daddy moved it because he was probably afraid you clumsy city slickers would let the animals out." Willy swung his stick at her playfully, and they began to trudge the half-mile or so across the field to Rocky Canyon.

As they approached it, Starrett could see the rocks that had given this creek and canyon their names. Geological activity over the eons had broken up huge layers of rock to create a formidable chasm that was rugged-looking, if not particularly deep. Only a hundred yards or so at its widest, the little canyon grew less rocky as it stretched away from them toward the Salmon River some four or five miles away to the west.

"I want us to hunt today in a way that Willy and I never have," Grace offered. "So, may I make a suggestion, Gar?"

"Fire away."

"Let's divide up the work. Why don't you take your detectors and check the flat rocks, crevices, gullies and other possible hiding places around the rim on this side of the canyon. With the detectors you can scan any areas where you suspect shallow digging could have buried the treasure. Willy can look for caves down below in the canyon itself, and I'll work around the edges and help both of you. As the same time, I'll be looking for any signs or markers that might indicate a treasure location."

"Great," Starrett said. "And, remember, Grace, you've got the most important job."

"How's that?" she asked.

"Looking for those signs," he reminded her. "Remember that we've decided that the treasure we're hunting must have been hidden in a hurry. And, the man or men hiding it didn't know when they'd be coming back . . . or, if they'd ever even have the chance to come back themselves. They had to leave some sort of sign that couldn't be easily changed . . . something that would last . . . and, something that could be described easily to others. Our research has shown us all of that. Now, while we're hunting, let's take advantage of this knowledge we've gained from research."

"Grace," Willy broke in, "look for something that appears to be natural, but isn't. It may be hard to notice without a little study. But, that's the way an Indian's mind will work. They'll try to leave something behind that *they* could notice easily but that you slow-witted white people would overlook."

"Good thinking, Willy," responded his wife, "even though the phrase 'an Indian's mind' is an oxymoron, if I've ever heard one!" Starrett chuckled, and Willy grudgingly joined in.

The three started hunting a mile or so downstream from where they had entered the canyon and worked back toward its closed end, nearer to Tolo Lake. Willy's truck was parked at the lake, and they planned to end the day's searching as close to it as possible. Remembering their own ideas about saving time and energy, they reasoned that any Nez Perce coming from the lake would not have walked too far before hiding the treasure.

Starrett searched along the top of the canyon and down into it, looking for rock piles and low spots. He carried with him two detectors, each of which he scanned occasionally. One was the Starrett Gold Hunter, especially designed to find precious metal, which he used most frequently. The other was a competitive instrument, a model equipped with a "double-box" searchcoil designed for ultra-deep hunting.

Starrett spotted numerous jumbled piles of rock, but he saw few in which a large treasure could have been quickly and easily buried. In passing Willy who searched down below, he commented, "Don't see many attractive possibilities. These rocks are too big, and they would have been too hard to move."

"Right," Willy replied. "Indians liked to hide caches in the big piles of slide rock that nature put on the slopes of long mountain faces. None of the rocks in those slides is particularly large, and you can dig deep into the pile pretty easily."

Starrett was finding little, but he enjoyed testing his company's new metal detector and comparing it with the competition. He was also surprised at the depth he was achieving with the computerized competitive model with the two-box attachment. He carried with him a gold nugget and several gold coins which he buried from time to time to test the effectiveness of his detectors in finding them. As the day grew warmer, he removed his jacket and leather vest and rolled up his sleeves. "Damn, but I enjoy treasure hunting," he exclaimed. "What a way to make a living!"

"What's that?" Grace yelled from up the canyon.

"Why don't we break for lunch," he answered

with a laugh.

As Grace unpacked the sandwiches and cooler of soft drinks they had brought with them, Starrett and Willy discussed the morning's activities.

"Lots of caves down there," Willy said. "But most of 'em are small, and I can't see any indication that makes one different from the other. It's hard for me to tell them apart, and I can't believe a Nez Perce would have left this treasure anywhere without indicating it some way. How are you coming in finding a surface marker, Grace?"

"No luck yet," she answered. "I think I understand what you're talking about, though, in looking for something that seems natural, but isn't."

Willy sat down his canned drink and turned to Starrett. "Speaking of unnatural things, there are paint marks on some of the rocks down there, especially the ones that are near entrances to the little caves. I've never seen them before."

"What do you mean, Willy?" asked Grace.

"Numbers and bullseyes scrawled on the rocks," he replied, "like someone was trying to keep track of the different caves. And, they must have been painted pretty recently."

"What colors?" asked Starrett.

"All the same . . . Sort of a dull orange," replied Willy. "You have any idea what they are?"

"Maybe," answered Starrett, as he arose. "Before we get started again, I want to thank you two for a great treasure hunt. I'm having a wonderful time!"

"How can you say that, Gar?" asked Grace. "We haven't found anything!"

"Not yet, Grace. Not yet." Starrett grinned. "But, all treasure hunts are wonderful . . . as long as nobody gets hurt or spends money he or she can't afford. When you find something . . . why, then your hunt becomes even more enjoyable."

Willy chuckled. "I guess that's one way to look at it."

"It's the only way to look at it," Starrett replied.

"Gar," began Grace, "I'm glad you brought up the treasure. We've never talked about what we would do with it, and you say in your books that partners should always decide about that before they find anything."

"You're right, Grace," answered Starrett, "except that's no problem here. Whatever we find belongs to you and Willy . . . and your father, I suppose, as landowner."

"No, Gar," broke in Willy. "You have to get . . ."

"Willy," interrupted Starrett. "you're already giving me a wonderful time up here in Nez Perce country, plus a chance to test my company's detectors and compare them with competition. If our discovery is a big one, I'll recover my out-of-pocket expenses, but that's all. And, I repeat what I said a minute ago, I already consider this treasure hunt an overwhelming success."

Grace and Willy could only smile as they walked away from Starrett, who was now busy changing searchcoils on one of the detectors.

Hours passed by as they continued searching, and the sun was setting before the three had reached the head of the canyon at its nearest point to Tolo Lake. Willy was among the rocks down in the canyon and Gar was on the opposite side when they heard a cry from Grace. She had walked back around the closed end of the canyon to the side nearer the old Indian campsite. "Come here quickly," she shouted. "I think I've found something."

Starrett laid down the detector he was testing and walked rapidly toward the young woman. She was standing on a spur of rock that extended out into the canyon, and he had to step across several small open spaces to reach her. Willy had an even more difficult time scaling the side of the canyon.

"Hey," they heard him shout, "there are a lot more of the orange numbers right down here."

Starrett finally reached Grace who stood silently and pointed toward the ground. He saw instantly what she had found – a large flat rock jammed vertically into a natural crevice. It appeared that the flat rock had sunk itself deeper as the fissure had widened over the years.

"Looks natural, but isn't," said Grace. "Right, Gar?"

"You've found a manmade marker, Grace," he

replied. "Nature certainly didn't leave one rock stuck at a ninety-degree angle in another one. Whoever put it there went to a lot of effort. That rock must be heavy!"

Willy pulled himself over the edge to join them and looked at the one rock stuck in another one. "It points down," he said. "Maybe the treasure is right below here in that cave."

"What cave?" Grace asked.

"The one I just found down below with some kind of *no admittance* sign stuck on the front of it!"

Chapter Nine

Neither Grace nor Starrett spoke. Both just stared at the scowling Indian.

"How can there be a sign on a cave?" demanded Grace.

"Let's go down and look," suggested Starrett in a quiet voice.

"There's a sign there," Willy replied urgently. "You'll see. And, you'll also see there's been a lot of activity near it recently. Footprints, and I can see where a lot of rocks have been thrown around."

Grace had already started nimbly hopping across the wide gaps formed by large, adjacent boulders as she worked her way down toward the floor of the canyon.

"I want you to look at the orange markers too," Willy added as he and Starrett scrambled slowly down the boulders. "The printed sign is in the same orange color, but I honestly didn't take time to read it."

Grace had hurried ahead of the two men, and by the time Starrett and Willie had reached the floor of the canyon, she was already looking at the colored numbers on the rocks and reading the prominent sign.

"H . . . S . . . R," she announced. "And here's what Willy described as a sign. It's a letter signed by something called the Historical Society of the Rockies. Darn, what if these research types have

beaten us to the treasure!"

Starrett pushed back his hat and placed his fists on his knees as he leaned over and silently read the sign. "Warns everyone to keep out," he said. "Says that a scientific party is exploring this area. Well, that's just B.S."

"What?" cried Willy.

Starrett pulled the sign from the rock, ripped it apart in the same motion and tossed the two pieces onto the ground.

"What are you doing, Gar?" exclaimed Grace.

"Haven't you heard of these frauds, Grace?" Starrett responded.

"I guess not."

"Well, there's no reason that you should have . . . not in a university library, at least."

"What's it all about, Gar?" Willy asked.

"H.S.R. is nothing but a bunch of rich amateurs down in Colorado who like to pretend they're archaeologists," he answered. "They've painted orange numbers all over the mountains from Montana to New Mexico and haven't done a damn bit of good from either from a scientific or historical viewpoint."

"What do they do!" Grace inquired with a shrill tone in her voice.

"Well, for one thing, they're always trying to keep legitimate treasure hunters off their so-called sites," Starrett replied. "Oh, they have a little museum they use as a tax write-off, and they'll issue credentials to anybody who asks for . . . "

"But, daddy would know about this!"

"Sure," Starrett responded. "Some idiots probably got in touch with H.S.R back . . . who knows how long ago . . . in the past. Then, the so-called society sent Rex a formal and harmless request on impressive letterhead . . . probably asked permission for a scientific expedition to search for Indian artifacts on his land."

"Oh, daddy would have approved that, I'm sure," Grace groaned.

"Right," continued Gar. "And, then . . . "

"But, just a doggone minute," Willy interrupted. "Nobody would have come snooping around out here without asking permission or, at least, telling Rex. Surely, that Society would require 'em to do that."

"Probably right, Willy," Starrett answered. "But, we have no idea who has these credentials. They're obviously not the type people who do as they're required or even think about asking permission.

"Probably some local fools, and we don't even have any idea who they are," Willy grumbled.

"Have you heard *anything* about it at City Hall or from the Chamber of Commerce?" Grace pleaded.

"Not a word," he replied. "And, I'm sure Rex would know, especially if the people had been decent and friendly."

"Or, scientific," Starrett added.

"Look at this sign," Willy picked up the two

pieces Starrett had tossed down and held them together. "It claims to be an Official Notice and says that the local representative of the Historical Society of the Rockies bearing credentials of the Society has been granted sole authority by the Society to search this area and that whatever is found becomes the property of the Society."

"Fancy language," Starrett snapped.

"Damn, damn, damn," muttered Grace. "Well, daddy can put a stop to all that."

"Right," Starrett said emphatically. "Their so-called Official Notice isn't worth the paper it's printed on. And, I'll help Rex with some calls to the Smithsonian and the American Museum."

Starrett stepped around her and crouched over to look inside the cave from whose mouth he had removed the sign. "I think we ought take a look ourselves now to try to find out what our accredited friends might have found while they were searching through this sole-authority cave of theirs."

"Before it gets any darker," Grace added, looking up at the canyon's rim.

"Let me go first with the flashlight and pistol, Gar," Willy said, "in case there are any snakes . . ."

"Or other unauthorized varmints," Grace added.

"You keep watch outside for us," Starrett said to the young woman. "No matter what the size of a cave or mine or no matter what condition you find it in, you never want your entire party in it and underground at the same time."

"Good idea," Grace replied. "Caves give me the creeps, anyway. I can't stand the thought of 'em. Probably full of bats!"

Willy grimaced, then then stooped to squirm through the low, narrow opening, closely followed by Starrett. They entered a surprisingly large room whose ceiling was considerably higher than the cave's mouth.

"Quite a cave," Starrett muttered as he followed the Indian who was shining his flashlight all around.

"You'd be surprised, Gar," replied Willy. "We get some interesting underground rock formations around here."

On the floor of the cave were indications of digging. Rocks that had been removed from a small hole lay strewn about. The large room sloped slightly downward toward the rear where the cave apparently continued into the darkness.

"Look, Gar," Willy said as he bent over and shined his light into the hole in the floor of the cave. "They got something out of a here that must have been covered with these rocks."

Instead, Starrett had directed the beam of his flashlight on the wall about five feet higher and was rubbing gently with the fingertips of his other hand.

"What's that you're looking for, Gar?"

"I don't know," he answered. "I thought I saw

some markings on the wall right above the hole . . . about head high. There are scratches in the rock, and I could see the shadows your flashlight made." Then, he laid his flashlight directly against the wall, permitting it to shine across the area where he had been rubbing.

"Look at this, Willy," he exclaimed. "Somebody has scratched something on this rock."

"Yeah, it looks like circles and arrows and a wiggly line or two," the Indian said as he leaned over to peer at the area illuminated by Starrett's light. "All of the lines are sort of connected, but they sure are faint."

"Could have been scratched in this rock a hundred years ago, huh?" Starrett observed, then pointed the light back toward the ground.

He stooped over and sifted his fingers through the sand and small pebbles in the depression Willy had been examining. "What's this?" he asked, lifting his hand and moving it in front of Willy's light.

He held a small piece of faded, worn leather.

"It's looks like part of an old bag, Gar," Willy stammered. "This could be old enough to have been part of a saddlebag that held the Nez Perce treasure. What do we do now?"

"Nothing more we can do today but get out of this damned cave," Starrett answered as he began crawling back out into the gathering dusk. "Then, we leave snake country before it gets too dark to see, and those rascals strike at the heat of our bodies."

As Willy explained to Grace what they had found in the cave, the two began glumly following Starrett who was leading the way across the pasture to Willy's truck.

"Uh oh," said Grace. "We have company."

And their vehicle had indeed been joined by a small, yellow Japanese pick-up, against which three large Indians were leaning.

Grace Erskine

I'm so mad I could spit. Those drunks trying to big-time Gar and tell him they were a scientific expedition. Exclusive rights to search my family's land . . . that's what they claimed they had. Even showed us some fancy-looking papers, and a letter from my father.

Exclusive rights. Just, dammitall!

I was afraid Willy was going to pull his gun and shoot them until Gar started laughing and tore up their papers. Then, I started laughing, and I thought Old Bareass would have a heart attack he got so mad and flustered. The other two were really drunk or so stoned out of their skulls that they hardly knew what was going on.

Gar ordered them to get off our property and said that he'd have the State Police on them if they trespassed again. Told them their fancy-language credentials were no good. Told them that since they liked big words so much, he'd give 'em some more to think about. How did he put it? Rendered null and void, effective immediately . . . *that's what he said about their credentials.*

Both of the other two were really stoned, but one was so far gone he kept mumbling and cursing. He was really out of his head, and we couldn't understand anything he said. Then, after they got in their little pick-up, the goofy one tossed something out the window at

Gar's feet.

We heard Old Bareass shout at him, telling him not to throw money away. But, then he leaned out the window at us and just grinned.

Told us we might as well get to keep a sample because **that** *was all we'd ever get.*

After the truck had spun off and thrown dust and pebbles in our faces, I bent over and picked up what they had thrown at us.

It was a dirty-looking old coin, which I handed to Gar. Then, I asked him what he thought it meant.

He poured some water from his canteen on the coin and as he rubbed it between his fingers, it began to shine more and more like gold. He polished it for the longest time. Then, Gar shook his head and smiled kind of sadly. He looked Willy in the eye, then me, before telling us what it was that the drunken companion of Old Bareass had thrown away . . . a very old gold piece.

Those three could have gotten it only from the missing Nez Perce treasure, *Gar said.*

Chapter Ten

Rex Thomas sat with his daughter and her husband in the restaurant across the street from the Grangeville motel where the young people were staying, along with Starrett. They had eaten breakfast and were waiting for their treasure hunting mentor to arrive while Grace described to the rancher all that happened the day before.

"I know," Thomas kept telling her, "Gar came by last night late, and we had a long talk. He's working on some things this morning. And, here he comes now."

Thomas nodded toward the door where Starrett was entering with several sheets of paper in his hands and a broad smile on his face.

"Our Nez Perce pal, Old Savage Fighting Grizzly Bear himself, has been dis-authorized by the HSR," he told the three, "and the HSR, meanwhile, has been kicked out of Rocky Canyon by Rex here and been warned by both the Smithsonian Institution and the American Museum of Natural History about its ethical practices."

"My, but haven't you been busy," Grace responded with a grin.

Starrett placed three sheets in front of Thomas. "Will you sign these, please, Rex?" he asked.

"Sure thing," the rancher replied as he wrote his name on each of the sheets. "What are they?"

"Just supporting letters for the telegrams you sent last night to New York, Washington and Colorado," Starrett replied.

"I sent, huh?" Thomas repeated. "Last night?" A quizzical look was on his face, but the hint of a smile betrayed his pleasure with Starrett's actions on his behalf.

"Have to keep those amateur diggers toeing the mark," Starrett commented. "They give professional archaeologists a hard enough time, not to mention us honest treasure hunters. But you don't want to get me started on that subject. I can talk all day!"

Willy spoke for the first time. "What we'd *like* to hear you talk about, Gar, are your opinions on what those drunks might have taken from the cave and where it leaves us."

"Did they find something?" Thomas asked. "What was it?"

"Nobody told you did they, daddy," Grace replied with a sly smile on her face.

"Take care of our breakfast check with this, will you, Rex," Starrett said as he pulled the shiny old gold piece from his pocket and handed it to Thomas, who studied it closely.

"Since we know that Grace's dad isn't interested in our foolish treasure hunting . . . " Starrett began. Then, he grinned as Thomas looked up from the coin in confusion. "We'll just leave him to his ranching, while we go back out to Tolo Lake to pick up where we left off yesterday. I'm convinced that our authorized historical researchers didn't even begin to find the treasure of the Nez Perce people."

"See you later, dad," Grace said as they walked away.

"We'll call you if we need a bigger truck, kemo-sabe," added Willy.

Thomas threw up his hands in surrender and tossed the gold coin back to Starrett as he called out, "I'll pay for breakfast with paleface money. Good luck!"

The ride back out to Tolo Lake was a short one, and Starrett did not begin sharing his ideas with Grace and Willy until they arrived at the old Indian campsite. When they left Willy's truck to walk across the pasture between the lake and Rocky Canyon, Starrett carried only the big stick Rex had given him the day before and his Gold Hunter detector. He quickly outlined the day's program of search to his companions.

"First of all, Grace," he began, "I'm convinced that the marker you found is the signpost left by the Nez Perce to lead them back to their treasure . . . "

"But, if they didn't hide it in that cave right below . . . " she argued.

"Be polite, dear. Let our guest talk," interrupted her husband. "I think Gar's got some Indian wisdom for us."

"Another oxymoron," quipped his wife, grinning. "But, seriously, where do you think the treasure is, Gar?"

"Somewhere else . . . nearby," he responded with a bland smile.

"That simple, huh?" replied Willy.

Starrett stopped walking, turned to the Indian and his wife and pushed back his battered hat. "Willy," he asked, "why don't you and Grace try to imagine yourselves hiding that treasure a hundred and ten years ago. What would you have done? Your first priority would have been just to hide it . . . safely . . . and in a good, secure place. Right?"

"I guess so," Grace replied haltingly.

"I see what you're getting at, Gar," Willy said. "The hiding place was the most important thing. You'd get the treasure put away safely before you even started thinking about marking the location."

"That's the way I see it," Starrett said. "The Nez Perce hid the treasure, then looked for a way to mark the spot. When they found a crevice to stick that flat rock into, they created the perfect permanent marker to indicate a location. They knew it would be there for a long time. But, their marker didn't necessarily indicate exactly where they hid the treasure. It just pointed down to the cave below it. Now, we're going to find out today about everything that's in that cave."

"How?" asked Grace.

"Willy and I are going to explore it more fully," Starrett answered, "while you wait outside."

"Okay," she pouted. "But, I don't like missing out on the fun!"

They began walking again toward the canyon, and Willy asked, "You don't expect that we'll find the treasure there . . . in that cave, do you, Gar?"

"No, I really don't," Starrett immediately responded. "But I'm always ready to be proved wrong. What I believe we'll find in that cave, though, are some pretty clear indications about just where the the gold is located. Some real clues! For instance, I want to study those marks over the spot where I believe Ugly Bear and his Indian pals dug up whatever they found."

"I'd rather not think about them," Grace said scornfully.

"Neither would I," replied Starrett, "and I hope we've seen the last of them. But, I'll bet you they didn't dig up very many of those coins like the one they tossed at us. In fact, I think the little bit they might have found was just left there as a teaser for whoever the Nez Perce might send later to retrieve their treasure. It would let them know they were on the trail of all the gold."

By now the three had reached the outcropping at Rocky Canyon where the marker was located, and they began climbing down the rocks to the cave opening at the bottom. Once again, Grace proved the most nimble.

"Lots of other caves around, aren't there, Willy?" Starrett asked.

"Yes," answered the Indian, "but they're a lot

smaller. Not many of those others are as easy to get into as this one. And, they probably aren't as large inside, either."

Starrett took the flashlight and metal detector into the large cave directly below the rock marker above. Before following him, Willy turned to his wife who had already sat down. "We'll be back in time for lunch, honey," he smiled. "Don't let anyone steal our lunch, and watch out . . . "

"For snakes!" she joined him.

Willy found Starrett holding his flashlight flat against the wall, trying to discern the markings clearly indicated by shadows cast by the beam.

"Markings are cut deeply into the rock, aren't they?" commented Willy.

"Had to be to last a hundred and ten years," replied Starrett. "Give me a hand, will you, Willy? Hold this light while I try to copy these marks."

"What do you think it could be, Gar?"

"Maybe just my imagination. The damned marks could be natural."

"No way," replied the Indian. "You've found some sort of map. The wiggly lines must be streams, but I don't know about the circles and arrows."

"Keep the light at an angle while I try to copy it," Starrett requested.

While Willy held the big flashlight, Starrett carefully reproduced the marks from the wall in a small notebook he took from his pocket.

"Now, let's check out the rest of this cave," Starrett said. "Scratching those lines, arrows and circles on the wall may just be what one of the Nez Perce did to kill time while the other ones buried the treasure. Or they might have been scratched on the rock a few thousand years ago while a glacier was dragging it along."

He shined his light around and jerked his head for Willy to follow as he began walking toward the back of the cave. As the ceiling became lower he had to remove his hat and bend over. But he continued edging onward as the floor sloped downward.

"What do you think, Willy?"

"Looks like it goes pretty far back . . . right on into the side of the canyon."

Willy was right. The floor sloped downward toward the rear of the room where it finally narrowed to a tight passage which Starrett examined. "Wait up, Willy," he said as he probed with his long stick into the opening. "Let me see where it goes before you try to follow . . . and I'll find out if it's big enough for a healthy fellow like you!"

In just a few moments he shouted back for the Indian to join him and to push the metal detector through the tunnel ahead of him. Willy was able to squeeze through and found himself crawling up into another room even larger than the one at the mouth of the cave.

"Hot damn," he exclaimed, "they must have hid it here. It's big enough."

"We'll see," Starrett responded. "I'll start scanning, while you look around. If the gold is in here, one of us will find it."

Neither did . . . despite an intense search by both for some two hours. Although the cave was cool, the men were perspiring when Starrett finally turned off his detector.

"Nothing here, Willy," he stated. "I've scanned over this entire room . . . the walls and even the ceiling, where I could reach it . . . in addition to the floor. And, you weren't able to locate any place where a treasure could have been buried or hidden behind or under rocks."

"Not a spot that looked suspicious, Gar," he answered, "and I sure . . ."

"What's that?" asked Starrett sharply. "I heard something."

"It's Grace," said Willy. "I can hear her calling from the front of the cave. Did you hear what she said? Damn, something must have . . . "

Willy's voice was drowned out by the thunderous sound of rocks falling. The noise came from the room where the two men had entered the cave. The earth shook, and a few small rocks fell from the ceiling of the area they had just searched. Dust billowed from the tunnel through which they had crawled up into this second room of the cave.

"Let's get out of here," Starrett commanded. "Quickly!"

Willy Erskine

What a mess! Grace in trouble and I'm trapped in this damned hole in the canyon and can't do anything to help her!

Gar managed to squeeze through the tunnel back up into the front room of the cave, but some rocks had shifted and it was too small for me. Kind of scary, being here alone with only a flashlight and Gar's detector to keep me company. Lucky for me the batteries were good!

But, Gar came right back with bad news. He told me that the entrance to the cave was blocked by rocks that had fallen down. He believes that it's the kind of accident that you can expect in an old mine or cave and that Grace has gone for help. I wish that were true, but I'm afraid this is no accident. All three of us need help . . . worse than he knows.

And, I don't think Grace has gone for help, either.

Because what I haven't told Gar yet . . . the last word I heard Grace scream was just that . . .

Help!

Chapter Eleven

Starrett didn't appear surprised or alarmed at Willy's report. He merely took off his hat and wiped the perpiration from his brow. Then, he nodded his head and muttered, "Damned fool Indians. They're in real trouble now," before pulling a book of matches from his pocket.

"You aren't a smoker, Gar," said Willy. "What are those for?"

"To get us out of here in a hurry," he replied and handed his flashlight to Willy. "We don't have time to wait for help. Shine both flashlights on the match when I strike it and watch closely what happens."

Starrett then extended his arms up in the air and waited for Willy to shift the lights upward before pulling a single match from the book and scratching it against the cover.

It was immediately blown out.

He repeated the procedure with the same results.

"What happened, Willy?"

"Wind blew 'em out!"

"Come on, dammit! Which way did the flame and smoke of the match blow?"

Willy's face brightened. "Oh, you think that a breeze from outside might . . . "

"Which way, I asked you."

"Sure," Willy said, and he shined the light

away from Starrett and pointed it up toward a pinched-in corner of the room. "Toward the ceiling on that side where the rocks are piled up."

"Let's climb up there and start digging," Starrett ordered.

The men climbed the pile of large rocks which they had searched so carefully just a short while before.

"I didn't notice any holes in the wall up here, Gar, did you?" asked Willie.

"No, but we weren't looking for a way up and out then," Starrett answered. "We were looking for a buried treasure cache."

They reached the top of the pile where it appeared that rocks long ago had fallen from the ceiling. Starrett struck another match, and it was immediately blown out.

"That way," Willie shouted, pointing to one side of the pile.

After only a few minutes of removing rocks from the spot Willy had indicated on the pile and throwing them down to the floor of the cave, the men saw daylight that signalled an escape from their prison. More than an hour of hard work passed, however, before they could move aside enough of the rocks for Willy to squeeze his bulk through the hole and join Starrett outside the cave.

"And, don't the fresh air smell good!" Willy exclaimed as he stretched his arms toward the sky. "Now let's go find Grace!"

Starrett was slapping his hat against his thigh to shake off the dust from the cave. Then he untied his scarf and wiped his face and neck with it. He had brought his big stick with him but left the metal detector behind inside the cave.

"Come on, Gar," Willy urged. "Let's go!"

"Where, Willy?" Starrett asked, looking steadily at him. "Let's not rush into any more trouble. I made a big mistake in leaving Grace alone this morning when we both went into the cave. I'm not going to misjudge our Indian friends again. I think General Howard must have made the same mistake a hundred and ten years ago. These three don't appear any more ready to give up than Chief Joseph was!"

"Don't compare them, Gar. Please don't."

"Just a figure of speech, Willy," Starrett answered. "There's no comparison."

"I just can't believe those three would have bothered Grace or tried to bury us in that cave," Willy exclaimed. "Man, that's heavy . . . Title Four, Chapter Two stuff!"

"What?"

"Oh, from the Nez Perce Law & Order Code," Willy muttered. "I just can't . . . "

"When a person gets his mind screwed up by dope or too much booze, Willy, there's no telling what craziness it can lead to," Starrett explained. "And, all the while, he thinks he's being logical and sensible. Those Indians are dead set on recovering that treasure."

"I know, Gar, but . . . "

"And they're ready to do just that to any of us who get in their way!"

"What's that?"

"Make us dead!"

The two men found that they were standing atop the edge of the canyon, but their movement underground had taken them some distance downstream from the marker that Grace had discovered the day before.

"Let's ease down into the canyon and edge back toward the mouth of the cave," Starrett suggested.

"Try to sneak up on anyone who might be there?"

"You got it, Willy," said Starrett. "So, let's keep quiet. But, get that pistol of yours ready!"

Wearing heavy boots, the two men found it difficult to move over the loose rocks without dislodging some of them. Each pebble that rolled down seemed to thunder like an avalanche. They continued to lower themselves slowly into the canyon, however, and finally reached bottom. Starrett gestured for Willy to take the pistol from its holster and lead them as they moved slowly back toward the cave where they had left Grace earlier that day.

In only a few minutes the two men were but a few yards away from the cave entrance which was just around the other side of a large boulder. Starrett placed one hand on Willy's arm to stop him, pushed back his hat and touched his lips with the other hand to indicate silence. Both men stood still and listened.

The noontime air of the canyon was heavy. Not a sound could be heard except the occasional call of a bird. Willy tilted his head forward, gestured with the pistol and raised his eyebrows to ask for Starrett's approval. He was answered by a curt nod.

With the pistol held before him the big Indian scrambled around the large rock, and Starrett could hear him say, "I'll be damned."

He quickly edged around the big boulder to join Willy.

"I heard you guys coming," replied the Indian known as Bareass who was sitting in front of the cave. He took a long drink from the can of beer in his hand, tossed the empty can out into the canyon and listened to its clatter. "What took you so long?"

Gar Starrett

First thing I have to do is keep Willy from shooting him!

Those other two must have taken Grace somewhere. So, she's probably all right. God knows, that one wouldn't have stayed around here if they'd pinned her under those rocks when they closed the cave up on Willy and me.

So, they've kidnapped Willy's wife. I guess he'd call that real Chapter Four stuff. And, I guess his Tribal Code would say that they attempted to murder us. Those three are crazy! At least, that one is . . . no question about it. But, we'll just have to wait him out to find out about Grace. I believe I know what he has on his mind . . . or, on what's left of it!

Willy Erskine

It all happened so fast!

I would have shot that son-of-a-bitch right off if it hadn't been for Gar. Then, I wanted to kill him, anyway, when he announced that the "tribe" was holding Grace "hostage" and wouldn't let her go until we revealed where "their" treasure was. Tribe, my you-know-what!

Like Gar had suspected, he and the other two found only a few coins in a small leather pouch buried in that cave. Gar being so smart, they decided . . . he must know right where the rest of the gold was. And, now he was going to lead them to it . . . if we ever want to see Grace alive again, that is!

The three of us just looked at each other . . . Bare-ass sitting on his butt . . . drunk and with a silly expression on his face . . . me, mad as hell . . . Gar, well, he was just looking around and fooling with that blue bandanna thing he wears. Seemed to be waiting for something. I think I know now what it was . . .

Since I'm certainly not going to ask, I'll probably never know if Gar could really see it coming. I'm not going to worry, either, about whether what he might have let happen was right or not. I just know that he put one arm around my shoulders from behind and told me to relax and stand completely still. Whispered that everything was going to be all right. You can't help but feel good around that fantastic self-confidence!

Then, he extended his other arm over toward Bare-ass with something in his hand. I couldn't tell what it was, but he asked him to come and get it . . . said we'd give him this map to the treasure, and they could let Grace go.

"Now, you talking sense, White Man," the drunken Indian grunted as he shifted his weight to rise from the ground. He stood and looked at Gar and me with an evil grin on that pudgy face.

From the way I was standing, I couldn't tell what it was that Gar had in his hand. It didn't look to me like the map I'd seen him draw. But, when I tried to turn around for a better look, I couldn't move. He was holding me tighter than I thought. Before I could speak again, Bareass had raised one foot to step toward us.

That's when the rattlesnake coiled behind the rock next to him struck and sank its fangs in his ankle.

Chapter Twelve

"Oh God, I'm snakebit!" the fat Indian screamed.

Bareass knew immediately what had happened. As he turned wildly to kick the snake away from his feet, he struck his knee sharply on the large rock and screamed again as he fell.

The snake struck at the Indian's arm and began crawling away as Bareass writhed on the ground, alternately sobbing and screaming out, "Shoot him, Willy! Kill the snake."

Willy had turned to point his gun at the rattlesnake, but Starrett stepped in front, brushing his arm away and shouting, "Quiet, all of you!"

Then, he stepped behind the large rock around which the snake had crawled. Willy and the Indian writhing on the ground watched as Starrett leaned forward on the long stick he had been carrying. He appeared to be pressing it hard against the ground.

"Willy," Starrett commanded. "Look over here and tell that rotten piece of scum what I'm holding for him with this stick."

Willy took a step toward Starrett and looked over the rock. His face froze in horror.

"Tell him, Willy."

"Bareass, Gar's got your rattlesnake."

The fat Indian lying on the ground shrieked in horror.

Willy breathed heavily and then laughed. "Yeah, he's got him a snake all right . . . I can tell it's the one that just bit you cause it looks sick to its stomach. Old Gar's got it pinned plumb to the ground with a forked stick." He laughed again. "Ain't that something!"

The Indian lying before him cried out and tried to rise. His knee collapsed and he fell down again moaning.

Starrett spoke. "You can tell him, Willy," he said, "that I'm going to bring this snake over and let it chew on his fat belly . . . "

"No," Bareass screamed. "No."

"Unless he tells us right now where Grace is and how we can get her."

Willy was standing over the other Indian who now lay sobbing loudly.

"You tell *me,* Bareass," Willy shouted. "Tell me quick, or, I'll gut-shoot you before Gar can drop that snake on you. Then we'll see which kills you first . . . lead poisoning or the snake's poison."

Willy kicked him hard in the stomach, and the fat Indian vomited and thrashed on the ground.

"Let him talk," Starrett said calmly. He was now standing next to Willy with the stick tucked under his arm.

He prodded the man on the ground with the stick, and the Indian gave an even louder squeal. "Where is she?" Starrett asked sharply.

"Over there," the Indian raised his arm and pointed down the canyon. "There's a cave about

25 yards that way, and she's tied up inside it . . . "

"There's no cave there!" Willy exclaimed and drew back his foot to kick again.

Bareass screamed, and Starrett restrained Willy.

"What about it?" he questioned, looking down. "You want some more of that snake?"

"No, no," the Indian screamed. "You got to believe me. It don't look like a cave . . . looks like a big rock sticking out of the mountain. But, get behind it, and you can see how to squeeze past real easy. There's a big cave there. It's where she's at. The rock's got our paint mark on it . . . number seven!"

"Who's with her?" Starrett asked.

"Nobody," the Indian replied, but Willy had already begun running down the canyon. As Starrett followed, he heard a scream from behind him, "For God's sake, don't leave me here with that snake. Don't let me die!"

Gar Starrett

It's no wonder that we missed it. That big rock with a "7" painted on it just blends right into the side of the canyon. It doesn't even look like you can get behind it! Willy went right on around it, though, and by the time I got there, was in the cave taking care of Grace. Apparently, they'd just tied her up loosely and gagged her. She would probably have gotten away before too long, but she was still a mess when we found her.

Sobbing . . . scared to death, and I don't blame her.

Two surprises. First, the other Indians were long gone . . . no sign of them. Second was the cave itself . . . a lot bigger than the other one. Didn't get much chance to look around. When I squeezed in, Grace's feet were still tied but her hands were already loose. She was crying in Willy's arms.

Grace Erskine

Thank God for heroes like Willy and Gar!

And, I almost don't care if that drunk dies. I'm even sort of glad he got bitten. All three of those nasty Indians had it coming to them!

Oh . . . that's terrible! I can't wish that on anyone. I'm just happy that it's all over.

A fine lookout I was! To be such big and fat people,

those drunken Indians can sure move quietly. They completely surprised me. I was sitting in the sun in front of the cave when they came right up to me. I wasn't paying any attention at all. Then, I tried to get inside . . . to yell and warn Willy and Gar, but they grabbed me before I could say very much. They had it all planned. One of them pushed just a few rocks, and the whole side of the canyon seemed to cave in. It was like they'd been expecting us, and I let them catch Willy and Gar in their trap.

It was awful. I just knew that Willy and Gar were dead or trapped in the cave . . . under tons of rocks. Then, the three of them took me to that other cave. I don't see how they ever found it, but they pushed me right inside and tied me up. From what I could understand, they had only stumbled onto it the day before and had never even been inside it before then themselves.

They were having a terrible argument. Sounded like White Bird and the other one were scared and didn't want any part of Gar and Willy. They had just been going along with Old Grizzly Bear. They begged him to let me go so they could all run away. They could see that they'd gotten themselves in deep trouble and it was only going to get worse.

Bareass was chattering like he'd lost his mind . . . just plain crazy. He couldn't stop talking about the Indian gold . . . was convinced that Gar had found it . . . kept telling the other two that it belonged to them and was trying to explain some involved plan he had for tricking Gar into giving him the location of the treasure. Then, once they knew where all the gold was located, he had another plan for leaving all three of us shut up in this cave. Ugh! Ordered those other two to guard me until he came back . . . told them to trap Willy and Gar if they came first. He was so arrogant when he strutted away. Then, the other two disappeared. I guess they just flat ran away as soon as he left. I think they were as scared as I was.

And, speaking of being scared, I honestly don't remember much after they left me in that cave. It was completely dark in there. I swear I could hear bats flying around, and I guess I was in shock. Then, when the screams and shouting started, I didn't know what to think. I couldn't even tell who it was, and I was so frightened for Willy and Gar. But, the next thing I knew Willy was untying me. Thank God for him . . . and, for Gar too.

I wonder if Gar really pinned down the snake and was going to throw it on that poor Indian. When I asked him, he just chuckled. Willy admitted he'd never actually seen Gar's stick holding the snake. Just told me that he said what he did because he thought Old Bareass had so many troubles then . . . one more would have been the coup de grace . . . a real sockdolager!

What a pair Willy and Gar are! They were so worried, but nobody hurt me. You think I could convince Willy of that? Boy, was he mad! And, he let that fat Indian know about it. With his leg and arm swell-

ing up, that crazy snake-bit fool nearly went out of his mind. I think he had decided we were going back to town without him. You should have heard his pitiful sniveling! Then, when Gar and Willy put him in the truck, he believed they were just going to dump him somewhere. Gar wouldn't do that!

With all the booze and whatever else he had in him, it's a wonder he didn't die before we got him to a hospital.

But-really-how-am-I-and-thank-you-very-much-for-asking . . .

Pretty good, to tell the truth . . . all things considered, that is. May not sleep too well for a night or two, but everything is going to be all right now . . . especially when we dig up the treasure . . . or uncover it . . . or whatever we do.

Gar's sure he knows where to find it!

Chapter Thirteen

"Are you sure, Grace," her father asked, " that you'll feel okay going back in that hole in the rocks?"

"Of course," she replied with a smile.

"Bats and all?" he asked, and she stuck out her tongue at him.

They were standing next to Willy and Starrett outside the mouth of the cave where Grace had been held prisoner just the day before. Starrett was carrying both his Gold Hunter detector which he had retrieved from the other cave and the competitive model with the double searchcoil deep-seeking attachment. Willy carried a shovel and a pick, and Grace had Starrett's camera bag slung over her shoulder.

"Why do you think we brought you along, daddy?" Grace teased. "I want to see what Gar and Willy find in there, and someone has to stand guard."

"Yeah," said Willy. "Stand guard! Remember that and watch out for those sneaky Indians. They've been known to creep right up on some slow-witted palefaces before you realize they're there!"

"Oh, you men are always ganging up on me," responded his wife.

"Not me," Starrett spoke up hastily with a slight smile on his face. He knew that they were all nervous because the treasure was foremost in everyone's thoughts. That gold coin had even finally gotten the attention of the rancher Thomas, and he had been eager to accompany them on this trip to Rocky Canyon. Starrett was convinced it would be the last trip he would have to make out here . . . one way or the other. This treasure hunt had reached the point of no return. If the treasure wasn't where he had decided it *should* be, then he had no idea of its whereabouts.

They'd soon find out!

"Go over that map for us again, please, Gar," asked Grace, "and tell us how you ever found it on the wall of that other cave?"

"Well, first of all, remember that it was Willy who decided it was a map," Starrett replied. "And I just happened to see its faint outline when we were shining our flashlights around that cave the first time. Never underestimate the value of luck in a treasure hunt! Now, we've got to work together to interpret it."

The day was beautiful with the sun high in the sky where they could see two hawks circling far above them. Down in the canyon there was no breeze and the air was warm. The four treasure hunters were too excited to be uncomfortable. Starrett opened his notebook. In it was the copy he had made from the wall of the cave located in the canyon just under the marker that Grace had found two days before.

"You think that big circle indicates Tolo Lake,

huh, Gar?" Willy asked, pointing to the edge of the drawing in Starrett's notebook.

"Yes," he answered. "But, our starting point has to be the arrow in another circle, and that arrow points down. I'm pretty sure this symbol indicates the marker that Grace found."

"The flat rock stuck in the crevice you showed me," Thomas said. "Back up the canyon and on the rim."

"Right," Starrett replied. "And, it's down the dry creekbed from the lake, as indicated by this arrow." He moved his finger across the small map.

"So, you believe those wiggly lines between the circled arrow and the Tolo Lake circle are the dry branches of Rock Creek?" inquired Grace.

"That's the way I read it," Starrett continued as he traced his finger along the lines on the map. "And, you can tell the direction of the flow because here's where the creek runs on into the Salmon River."

"But the rock marker on the edge of the canyon is the key, huh?" questioned Thomas.

"Sure," answered Starrett, "That's what the Nez Perce who hid the gold would want the others to be looking for when they came back to recover it. That would point them to the cave below with this map in it. They'd know they found it when they dug up the small bag of coins out of the floor of the cave in front of the map."

"What about those other circles and arrows," asked Willy.

"I believe that the next circle . . . the one below the circled arrow . . . indicates the cave where this map was scratched on the wall," Starrett answered. "The little circle inside that circle must symbolize the bag they buried there . . . the one with just a few gold pieces in it. Then, the next arrow points downstream to still another circle with a smaller circle inside it. That's got to be this cave . . . old Number Seven . . . the one that has the rock completely hiding it."

Willy moved to the back of the rock in front of the cave, waved his hand at the narrow entry space behind it and said, "So, where is the treasure . . . inside there?"

"This final arrow is bent," Grace pointed out. "The one under the last little circle. It's also inside the big circle that stands for this cave, Look how it points up."

"And, I believe we'll find that it points up to some sort of shelf high inside the big room of that cave," Starrett said. "I didn't have time to look for it yesterday, but . . ."

"With Bareass handcuffed to a hospital bed, the other two Indians in jail and Rex here to stand guard, we're all going to look," Willy added. "Right, Gar?"

"Let's go," he said, and the three began squeezing into the cave.

As he watched them enter, Thomas shook his head and murmured, "I'd never of believed a cave was back there." Then, he shouted, "Good luck!"

Grace, the final one to enter the cave, answered him with a smile before she disappeared inside.

In addition to the two detectors that Starrett carried and Willy's pick and shovel, each had a large flashlight. As they shined them around to examine the cave thoroughly, the beams flitted over its ceiling and traced bizarre patterns of light and shadows on the jagged rock faces. After a few seconds their search for some sort of shelf or ledge became more organized. Starrett paced carefully around the walls of the cave and shined his light directly upward. Grace and Willy stood in the center of the cave and methodically moved the beams of their lights around the ceiling of the cave where it met the walls.

"Oh, darn, I don't see a thing," moaned Grace. "I thought it would be so easy!"

Starrett stopped pacing around the walls of the cave. "If I could leave everyone with just a thought or two about treasure hunting," he said, "the first would be that it's *seldom* easy. From the dedicated research before each search through the effort of the hunt itself, it's most often hard work."

"And, sometimes dangerous, too," Willy snorted.

"What's the second thought you'd tell everyone about treasure hunting, Gar?" Grace asked.

"I'd tell them that hunting for treasure with a metal detector is the most fulfilling and rewarding hobby in the world!"

"Well, I wish we could find *our* treasure," Grace wailed.

Starrett grinned as he walked to one side of the big room and raised his arm to indicate its upward slope. "It may be up there," he indicated. "Why don't both of you climb up and tell me what you find."

"Up that wall?" Grace asked. "How?"

"If you look closely, you can see that it slants pretty sharply," Starrett replied. "I don't think either of you will have any trouble . . . especially you, Grace, with those sneakers you're wearing today."

"What are we looking for," Willy asked.

"Just climb up that sloping wall as high as you can," Starrett replied. "Tell me what you find."

Grace and Willy immediately began scaling the wall. Wearing boots, Willy moved awkwardly behind his wife who scrambled ahead of him. She stopped when she heard Willy yell, "Watch out . . ."

"For snakes," she completed his warning, then stopped and waited for her husband to reach her halfway up what they realized was, indeed, a sloping side of the cave. She squeezed his hand, and they continued on all fours along and up the slope a few feet to where the wall appeared to reach the ceiling.

"Hey," Willy shouted, "look what's here!" As Starrett watched, the couple bowed their heads and seemed to disappear mysteriously between the wall of the cave and its ceiling. Willy's head popped back out, and he said, "You'd better bring your detectors on up, Gar. It's not a ledge like we expected. but there's another room up here with a floor of loose rock . . . looks deep enough for something to be buried in it."

"Better bring the digging tools too, then, hadn't I?"

"I'll come down and help," shouted Willy as he began scrambling and sliding along the wall.

When he reached bottom, Willy picked up the two detectors to help Starrett take them up. He was obviously surprised at their light weight, even the competitive model with the large deepseeking searchcoil. "Easy to handle, aren't they, Gar?" he remarked.

"Willy, I couldn't sell a detector unless it was light and easy to manage," Starrett answered as they climbed the sloping wall together. "When you spend the whole day out in the sun and wind . . . or confined in a cave, like we are . . . you aren't going to burden yourself with a detector that's heavy or clumsy."

They lowered their heads and went down between the space at the very top of what had appeared a wall that extended to the cave's ceiling. "How'd you know this was up here, Gar?" Willy asked.

"It was sort of an optical illusion," he answered. "When you look closely, you can tell that both the floor and ceiling slant and there's really nothing close to a right angle in this cave. The shadows made by all of our lights flashing around helped me see that there was some sort of space between where the wall appeared to join the ceiling. So, you and Grace climbed up and found . . . what?"

"Just lots of rocks," replied Grace, who was idly picking up stones and casting them aside. There were enough to keep her busy because the entire floor of this upper room of the cave appeared to be filled with rocks no larger than good-size walnuts. The room was at least twenty feet long by ten feet wide with a ceiling nearly high enough for Willy to stand erect.

"Hold it, kid," Starrett commanded gently. "Don't muss up your pretty hands. Let me scan around here for a while first, and we'll ask Willy to dig up what we find."

Starrett laid down his crumpled hat, put on earphones and picked up the detector with the two large square searchcoils. "We need to look deep down in these rocks," he explained, "so I'm going to use this detector with a deep-seeking Bloodhound searchcoil. It's made by Garrett, but no other manufacturer has anything like it. Hooking up this Bloodhound makes this new, computerized Garrett detector the deepest seeking there is. Besides, the Bloodhound is by far the easiest and most accurate of all the two-box searchcoils to use."

For several minutes Starrett scanned the detector over the rocks on the floor of the room. He went back and forth across the entire area several times, stopping occasionally to push some rocks aside with his foot. Finally, he removed the earphones, laid his detector down and pointed to one of the rocks he had moved. "Let's dig here, Willy."

After they had used the tools to move aside enough rocks to make a hole some three feet deep, Starrett called out to Grace, "Bring me that other detector, will you, please."

"This is a Starrett detector that we call the Gold Hunter," he related. "If there's gold down there, this instrument will indicate it. We use a circuit that's been proved reliable all over the world. There's no question that this is the best detector ever made for locating gold."

He then donned earphones again and began scanning his detector around in the large hole he and Willy had dug. Shortly, he removed the earphones, laid down the detector and spoke quietly to Grace and Willy who were kneeling beside the hole.

"Listen to this," he said. Starrett then unplugged the earphones from the detector and again began to lower its searchcoil down to the bottom of the hole.

"What are we listening for?" Grace asked.

"Something to keep the bats away," Willy said as he mussed her hair lightly.

Grace slapped Willy's hand gently while Starrett continued lowering the detector until its searchcoil neared the bottom of the hole he and Willy had dug. The speaker of the detector began emitting a sharp buzzing sound which grew louder as the searchcoil descended.

As Starrett turned up a control knob on the detector, the sound grew even louder in volume until it echoed and resounded throughout the cave.

Grace clapped her hands over her ears.

"What *is* that sound, Gar?" Willy shouted.

Starrett lifted the detector from the hole and flipped a switch. The noise ceased abruptly.

"It's the most beautiful sound in the world, Willy," he replied. "It's the sound made by the missing Nez Perce gold. Want to join me in digging it up?"

Grace Erskine

I guess all of you, by now, have some idea of what it was that Willy and Gar dug up . . . at least, you do if you saw that story in the magazine with all the pretty pictures. Gar took a lot of color slides of the treasure and of us and everything else around there. Then, the magazine sent out some photographers, and daddy wouldn't let the guards admit them to the property. Said he had to call Gar to make sure their credentials were real. We all had a big laugh over that.

It's too bad about those three Indians. The snakebite didn't kill the big one, but doctors decided that Old Whatshisname had pretty well fried his brain with dope, and they sent him off to an institution. When the other two promised to leave here and never come back, we suspended pressing any charges. The police promised us they would arrest either of them if they ever showed up around Ruger or anywhere in Northern Idaho again.

About what we found . . . we really aren't ready to say anything more yet. Coin collecting experts have warned that it's possible we could even seriously depress the price for certain gold pieces . . . worldwide. It's hard to believe that we found that *many! But, you saw the pictures in the magazine . . . all those down in that hole Willy and Gar dug . . . and that was just the* top *of it. I can only tell you that the Nez Perce treasure is fabulous and that Gar Starrett is a fantastic man for helping us find it and for saving my life.*

Without him, of course, we never would have located the treasure. I don't care what nice things he said about us in that magazine article. If it hadn't been for Gar, Willy and I not only would have never found the treasure but probably would have gotten both our fool selves killed . . . one way or the other! Those other Indians would be in prison now, and the treasure would be missing for another hundred and ten years!

Gar Starrett

What a delightful treasure hunt it was! But, then, aren't they all. If nobody gets hurt or spends money he or she can't afford, every treasure hunt is a genuine pleasure . . . especially when we find something.

It's up to Willy and Grace to announce precisely what we found. It certainly all belongs to them since the treasure was on Rex's land, and nobody can prove who buried it . . . even though Willy and all of us have a pretty good idea. Willy is on the right track though! He intends to use the money to help young Indians in this area and around the Northwest. Improve local schools . . . make them the best in the country . . . that's his first goal. Then, provide scholarships to anyone who'll go on to college. Nez Perce, to start with . . . then, the other tribes. All the while, trying to create new job opportunities in this area. He's already working with excellent consultants. Their results should be something to watch!

Maybe he'll even loan a few coins for an exhibit at the HSR Museum!

Willy and Grace are wonderful people. This area is lucky they've chosen to keep living here . . . and even luckier that they kept searching for the Nez Perce treasure!

And, I was pretty fortunate myself to be able to help them after she found the rock marker and Willy pointed out the map that helped us all locate The Missing Nez Perce Gold.

A Closing Note

Much of what you have read concerning the search for the missing Nez Perce gold is true. I know, because I helped look for it. In fact, I was with Gar Starrett's friend Roy Lagal when he – not the lovely, shapely and entirely fictional Grace Erskine – found the large rock wedged vertically in a crevice on the rim of Rocky Canyon near Tolo Lake. I vividly remember Roy motioning for me to come to him as he shouted across the canyon, "Charles, here it is . . . I've found it!"

Was this big rock left by some member of the Nez Perce tribe in 1877? I believe that it was. I'll assure you that the wedge-shaped rock is every bit as big and well lodged in the crevice as it appears in the photograph on the back cover of this book. This was how the rock still looked in the late summer of 1988, many years after we first discovered it. You can look at it on the north side of the canyon very near the closed end and on an overhang . . . just where Grace "discovered" it in the novel!

And, caves in the rock lie just below this marker, just as "discovered" by Grace's husband, Willy!

It would be remiss of me not to admit that the study of the Nez Perce and their history has been a favorite hobby of mine for many years. I have visited the area numerous times and cherish the many friends I have made there. To all of them, I say that if you try to find yourself in this story, you won't. All characters since the days of Chief Joseph are completly fictitious . . . except for Roy Lagal, whose friendship, advice and counsel have been invaluable in preparation of this novel. And, my Nez Perce friend of many years, Wally Eckard, served as the inspiration for Willy in our story.

Of course, I am not aware of any such institution or organization known as or resembling the Historical Society of the Rockies. I apologize if anyone feels toes being stepped upon here. It was not intentional.

When our search party investigated the area below the rock that we believe was left by the Nez Perce, however, we *did,* indeed, find painted signs that included the markings of a museum society. Because it was one of the major international institutions, we restricted our search efforts and did not examine any marked caves. Unlike Grace, Willy and Gar . . . we found no treasure. The discovery described in this narrative with its resulting magazine article is entirely fictional . . . unfortunately!

More about the museum group we encountered: later investigation revealed that the institution in question had no record of any of its representatives searching or conducting any operations in the Rocky Canyon area.

Who left the painted markers? Once again,

your guess is as good as mine.

Is the Nez Perce gold still hidden somewhere in Rocky Canyon near Tolo Lake, just west of Grangeville? I am convinced that it is, just as I am convinced that the rock marker that Roy found offers the principal clue to the whereabouts of this treasure.

Before you pack up your Bloodhound and Grand Master Hunter to head for Idaho, remember that the canyon is located on private property (not owned by Rex Thomas, either!) where aggressive bulls have been known to roam around.

One final note about the other animals and reptile(s) of our novel. We did encounter bats near the entrance to one cave, and I have seen far more rattlesnakes in Idaho than in my home state of Texas. So, look out for them!

If you decide to seek The Missing Nez Perce Gold, good hunting! Gar and I will *see you in the field . . .*

Charles Garrett